It's not about Sha⌋

It's not about Shakespeare

Aspects of ordinary life in Stratford-upon-Avon 1775-1915

Val Horton

YouCaxton Publications
Oxford & Shrewsbury

ISBN 978-1-912419-76-0

Printed and bound in Great Britain.
Published by YouCaxton Publications 2019

YouCaxton Publications

enquiries@youcaxton.co.uk

To Christopher and Simon Horton

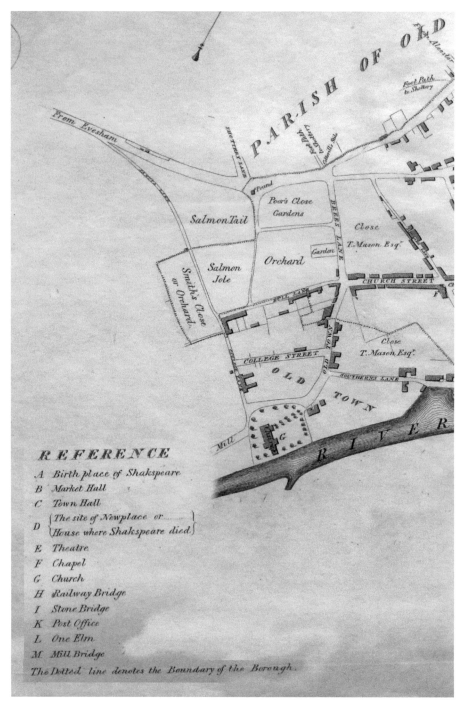

REFERENCE

A   Birth place of Shakspeare
B   Market Hall
C   Town Hall
D   { The site of Newplace or
     { House where Shakspeare died }
E   Theatre
F   Chapel
G   Church
H   Railway Bridge
I   Stone Bridge
K   Post Office
L   One Elm
M   Mill Bridge
The Dotted line denotes the Boundary of the Borough.

Fig 1. Map of Stratford-upon-Avon c.1830 showing street names

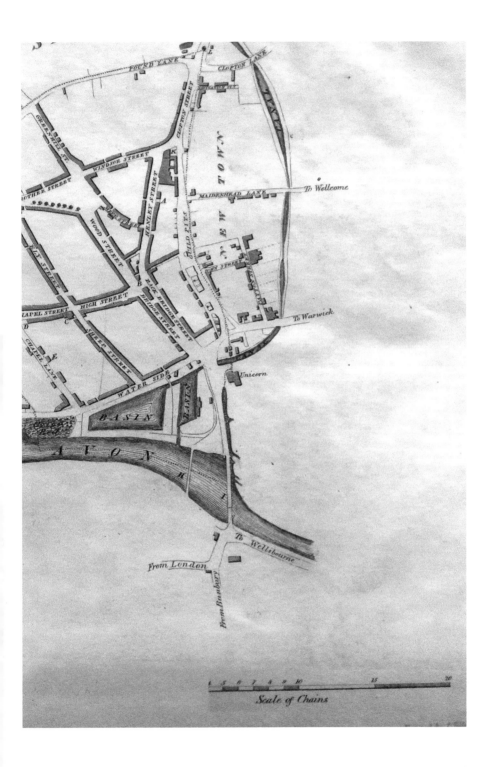

Scale of Chains

Acknowledgements

I wish to thank Pat Loe, my husband, for his invaluable and wide ranging support from the very start. My thanks also go to friends, Judith Ellis for reassuring me when it seemed impossible and the late Sheila Stephens whose early encouragement really kicked it all off. Thanks also to Laurence French, a friend of a friend, whose very bright idea meant I took the plunge and had a go at publishing. Thank you all so much.

It is a pleasure to acknowledge the important work, accomplished by two volunteers at the Shakespeare Birthplace Trust (BPT), my local archive, Norma Hampson and Cyril Bennis. Their input has enabled me to give colour and detail that would otherwise have been impossible.

Finally, a big thank you to the staff of the BPT Reading Room who were incredibly helpful to reader 3410. The title of this book is a playful reference to them. It is almost the phrase they say when members of the public see the wealth of local history to be found in the archives that is *not* about 'the life and times of William Shakespeare'.

Contents

List of Illustrations

All illustrations are courtesy of *The Shakespeare Birthplace Trust* unless stated otherwise.

Foreword

When examining the history of a town, a writer will often search initially for a narrative structure that describes its development. When that is established, he or she will then fill out this simplified narrative with details based on research in local archives. The broader narrative comes first; the details follow, and the town itself is the hero or villain of the piece. Indeed some local histories are even titled explicitly 'XXXton the Biography'. It's a handy way of telling the story and can make history accessible and comprehensible.

This book is different. It works the other way round; it starts with the particular and from that implies the broader narrative. The result is a fascinating glimpse into Stratford's past, a complex history made up of the intertwining stories of individual inhabitants of the town, people who are uncomfortably and recognisably similar to ourselves today, both in what motivates them and in their triumphs and failures. There is greed, betrayal, disappointment, success, kindness, complacency, arrogance and despair, just as we experience such things today. Of such is Stratford made.

Val Horton's impressive research in the Stratford archives has unearthed the tortuous financial and business transactions behind the development of Mayfield Avenue to the north-east of the town centre, starting with inclosure of the original fields back in the late eighteenth century and with the machinations of Mr John Keen, a wealthy maltster intent on self-enrichment. From this narrow but fascinating base it traces succeeding generations of the various families who had an interest in the land and expands outwards to look at broader social developments, such as the extension of the franchise, the development of hospitals, and the position of women. We are thus able to see these broader developments through the eyes of contemporaries, eyes which were focussed first and foremost on themselves and their own interests - just as today we are subject to the broad currents of history even as we live our own lives.

It has been a great pleasure to work with Val on this book and I have myself learned much in the process. Of one thing I am certain: I would not wish it that some future historian should dissect my own dealings with Val's forensic attention to detail - not that I have much to be ashamed of, but because we all of us, I suspect, look remarkably similar when exposed to such levels of scrutiny.

Bob Fowke, Editor, YouCaxton Publications

Introduction

This book is about past life in Stratford-upon-Avon, a small town made famous as the birth (and death) place of William Shakespeare. This connection to the famous playwright has caused an ever-increasing flood of visitors from all parts of the world. Many come with the intention of paying homage to the revered bard whilst others stumble off the coach and accidentally find themselves doing much the same anyway. Possibly because of this compelling connection other important aspects of Stratford's history have been sadly neglected.

I discovered this to be the case whilst searching in the local archives. I was there to find out more about a particular Edwardian house and was hopeful that I could write just a short piece about it as a keepsake for my two sons who grew up there. It would have been a slim affair about an extraordinary Victorian woman called Jane Edwards who was responsible for building it. There the book was to end. But Jane Edwards had a dream that involved not just one house but many more. To make it all happen she needed land, and a lot of it. It was 1881, following a fierce battle, when she finally had it all. In revealing her struggle the archives led to a host of other local characters who had gained ownership of her precious land in earlier years, some happily and some less so. All saw it as a means of making money but for John Keen, the first owner (following an Act of Inclosure), and Jane Edwards the land held a particularly powerful interest. By investigating the 140 years between Keen's acquisition in 1775 and Jane Edwards' death in 1915 a great deal of Stratford life has been revealed. Spanning the reigns of George III, through to Edward VII, it necessarily covers a period of remarkable change.

Chapters in the book are divided. Details of the land and the house can be found in the odd-numbered chapters whilst details of Stratford life can be found in the even-numbered chapters. All the characters involved are ordinary people of Stratford and on occasions it has been possible to use their own words; they may not be as well-chosen as

Shakespeare's but they do have a clarity that we can appreciate today. A furiously angry George Cope leaving a local pub armed with a poker and shouting 'damn my eyes if I don't murder somebody with this before I have done with it', is one example among many. There is also much that is poignant. We can feel sadness for Mary Coggins and her long life in the workhouse and for the fall of the respected Warrilow family, and it is touching to witness the sympathetic words of a JP towards Albert Danks and his stolen duck. These events may not have been played out with quite the drama of Macbeth or King Lear but they touch the heart and mind. Perhaps the ordinary people of Stratford-on-Avon were not quite so ordinary after all.

The source material for this book is almost exclusively derived from the archives of the Shakespeare Birthplace Trust. As a complete novice in the area of historic research (any research) I thoroughly enjoyed the challenge of the process but I have to acknowledge that there may be omissions and possibly mistakes and, if you notice any, please contact me so that a correction can be made.

Plan of Stratford upon Avon showing properties of interest

The numbers on the right below give the chapter in which the buildings first feature.

1	Stratford Board School	14
2	Trinity College	14
3	The Infirmary	16
4	Guild Hall School	14
5	Mr Austin Warrilow's school	14
6	Mr John Fetherston's pub	11
7	Russell Court	18
8	The Police Station	10
9	The Town Hall	4
10	The 1892 Post Office	8
11	The Nursing Home & Sick Children's Hospital	16
12	Miss Fanny Payne's home	12
13	The National Schools	14
14	Stratford-upon-Avon Hospital	16
15	The Labourers' Dwelling Company Ltd housing	18
16	The Labourers' Dwelling Company Ltd housing	18
17	The Suffragists' shop	20
18	George Durant's shop	17
19	The second Post Office	8
20	Jane Edwards' Bridge Street shop	19
21	The Newland's shop	13
22	Miss Mary Newland's alms-houses	13
23	Mr Henry Bullard's yard	4
24	Jane Olney's first guest house	Appendix 4
25	The Labourers' Dwelling Company Ltd housing	18
26	Jane Olney's second guest house	Appendix 4

Fig 2. Plan of Stratford-upon-Avon showing properties of interest

To Warwick

N

BASIN

BASIN

ON

To Shipston

27	The Petty Session House & Police Station	10
28	John Keen's house	1
29	Jane Olney's Henley Street shops	Appendix 4
30	The Corporation Workhouse	12
31	St Gregory's School	14
32	The first Post Office	8
33	William Durant's Henley Street houses	17
34	The White Lion Inn	2
35	Miss Maria Coggins' home	12
36	Jane Edwards' Mulberry Street houses	11
37	Mr Fred Winter's toy factory	22
38	William Durant's four shops	17
39	The Union Workhouse	12
40	The Infectious Diseases Hospital	16
41	Mrs Lucy Sheasby's home	22
42	'Elm Cottage'	11
43	Jane Edwards' houses, 32 & 34 Maidenhead Road	19
44	William Durant's houses 36 & 38 Maidenhead Road	17
45	Jane Edwards' house 40 Maidenhead Road	19
46	Jane Edwards' house 42 Maidenhead Road	19
47	Jane Edwards' house 1 & 2 Mayfield Avenue	19
48	Ann Edwards' houses 3, 4. 5 & 6 (land) Mayfield Avenue	23
49	Ann Edwards' land sale (7)	23
50	Jane Edwards' houses 8, 9, & 10 Mayfield Avenue	23
51	William Durant's houses	17
52	Jane Edwards' land sale (10a)	23
53	Jane Edwards' houses 11 & 12 Mayfield Avenue	23

Chapter 1

Mr Keen & Inclosure

The story of 5 Mayfield Avenue begins in 1775 with Mr John Keen and an Act of Inclosure. Local archives tell of possibly several John Keens living in the locality at this time. There was a very wealthy maltster, a wool dealer, a book dealer and a yeoman. Mayfield Avenue's John Keen was certainly the maltster (he produced malt for brewing). He is known to have owned land scattered in the Old Stratford, Bishopton and Welcombe areas along with handsome houses set in the very heart of town. When Parliament passed Stratford's Act of Inclosure and the Commissioners arrived to meet with the landowners, he was one of the wealthy few who were able to choose exactly what land they wanted. It had not been easy; to get to that point there had been incredible anger, upset and double dealing amongst the town's wealthy.

Inclosure so radically altered Stratford that it warrants explanation. It set the scene for all that was to follow. Before inclosure people living in and around town had certain rights with regard to the common land; they had the right to pasture, pannage, marl, estovers and turbage. This entitled them to let their cattle, sheep and horses graze there (pasture), turn their pigs out in autumn to eat nuts there (pannage), dig for sand and gravel (marl), collect fallen wood and small bushes (estovers) and cut turf for their fires (turbage). These activities were of great benefit to poor families. Additionally, the surrounding open-field farming meant that there were many farmers, both large and small, with strips of land scattered in the large open-fields. After inclosure this changed. The common land virtually disappeared and the old system of strip farming was replaced by private ownership. Small farmers were driven off the land and those remaining found their already harsh lives made even harsher.

Inclosure had been happening around the country since the twelfth century but, until the eighteenth century, it was on a much smaller scale and did not always involve Parliamentary intervention. Between 1750 and 1860 the rate of inclosures was at its highest. There were several reasons for this. One view, expressed by historians of a Marxist persuasion, is that the land was appropriated by the rich in order to create a landless class who were then available to work in the new factories. For many people, especially the poor, inclosure was seen as robbery on a grand scale: why alter a system that worked for the benefit of the majority? But others saw it as both a good and inevitable change: by relinquishing the old way of farming and by creating undivided fields it was possible to produce enough cheap food for the rapidly growing urban population. After inclosure, recently improved agricultural techniques could be fully implemented, something that many landowners had wanted for some time. In Stratford it was not going to be an easy transition.

When inclosure became an important local issue, Mr Keen, the maltster and landowner, was a comfortably-off family man living in a small town with a population of just under 1,300. He lived in Henley Street in the house next to the building that was once Shakespeare's home (Fig 2 No. 28). He would have mingled with other landowning gentlemen who, over the years, were to attend many meetings to debate the pros and cons of inclosure. The first of these meetings was called in 1766, the invitation being sent out on the evening of the 14th December (Fig 3). It came from two men, Mr Harrison and Mr King, and it went to the Mayor, members of the Corporation and all 'the proprietors of lands in Stratford and Bishopton'.

Mr Harrison and Mr King wished to consult about the 'properest means of obtaining an Act of Parliament this sessions for Inclosing the Open Fields'. The meeting was to be held at the White Lion Inn, situated in Henley Street, the following morning at 10 o'clock. It is probable that Keen attended this meeting. The notion that a meeting could bring about inclosure for 'this sessions' of Parliament was staggeringly wide of the mark.

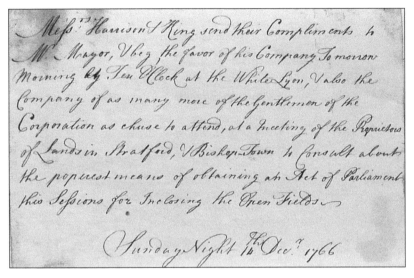

Fig 3. An invitation to consider inclosure 1766

Opposition

It would seem that feathers had been ruffled among those with influence. There were powerful men in favour of inclosure but there were also many others who opposed the notion. Ten days after the December meeting a second meeting was called which expressed opposition to the whole idea and produced a strongly worded petition. This 1766 petition stated that the 'Proprietors of land in the open and common fields… do declare that we are unwilling that the said fields shall be inclosed… and will oppose such inclosure as far as we lawfully may or can, and pay the Charges and Expenses that shall attend such opposition'.[1] Since Keen's signature is not one of the thirteen, it may be assumed that he was in favour. He was one of the largest landowners and would have believed it to be in his own best interest. He was not alone in coming to this conclusion.

At another meeting, votes were simply recorded (Fig 4) with those attending rejecting any change. There was a flurry of further meetings when interested parties connived to get the decision they wanted. Five long years later, in December 1771, Mr Thomas Mason penned a note to interested parties referring to an exercise he had suggested the previous year: to commission a 'skilful and honest man' to value the lands in order to determine whether inclosure would be beneficial.[2] Mr Mason saw this as a sensible and practical way forward to end the conflict. The survey that Mr Mason proposed was commissioned, and Mr William Smith and Mr Manley Ashwin were appointed in

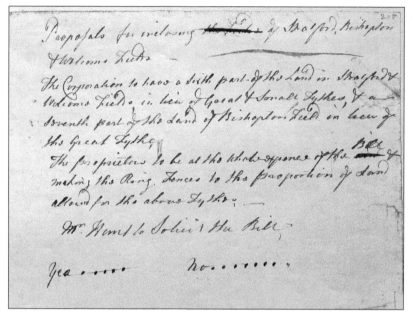

Fig 4. A vote that went against the whole idea (undated)

January 1772. That same year, and tired of the whole business, seven men, including Mr Keen and Mr John Payton, took a petition to Parliament urging a Bill be prepared as presently their 'lands and grounds are inconveniently situated'. They were stopped in their tracks by two men, Mr John Partheriche and Mr Hobbes, who were outraged that they 'did not cause a meeting of the proprietors, as it would not serve their purpose for they know a majority is against it'.[3] The seven must have been furious as the law was about to change and not in their favour. In future, any petition would have to include the signatures of the majority of people affected.

In the middle of this mayhem Mr Smith and Ashwin diligently measured the land and presented their Survey of Stratford in December 1773.[4] They concluded that to create twenty-acre fields and fence them would cost £510. The expenses of the commissioners would be £230, which together brought the total to £740. This must have spurred matters on for at a public meeting held on the 26ᵗʰ January 1774 all twenty-three attending (including one woman) voted for inclosure. Even Samuel Smith who had it recorded that he had promised Mr Partheriche he wouldn't. Those against were notably absent. Seven men present were charged with managing the process.

But the fight was not over yet. In 1775, a total of twenty-six influential men sent a last-ditch petition to Parliament expressing their great concern and opposition to inclosure. They 'humbly pray that they may not be compelled to alter the Present mode of Enjoyment of their respective properties' it would be 'detrimental and Injurious to their respective interests'.[5] This unsuccessful petition contained surprises. Included were the names of Simon Cale, Samuel Morris and James Keating who had signed the 1772 petition sent to Parliament requesting a Bill be prepared. It was too late; their petition failed to stop what must have seemed, by then, inevitable.

Implementation

Following the presentation of the successful petition, and Parliament's subsequent award in 1775, enforcement moved at a rapid pace. The rules, set within the law covering inclosure, were clearly laid out and wheeling and dealing was not an option. The printed Act stated that the lands to be inclosed 'are reputed to consist of Fifty Yard-lands or thereabouts, besides some odd-Lands, and which do contain in the Whole by Estimation One thousand Six hundred Acres or thereabouts'.[6] By way of an introduction the Act informed all, who cared to read it, that the present lord of the manor was the Duke of Dorset and it named the five largest landowners, the largest landowner being Mr John Payton, proprietor of the White Lion. It concluded that other owners of small 'parcels of land intermixed and dispersed' were often subject to 'frequent trespasses and much inconvenience' and therefore inclosure was going to be beneficial for most landowners.

The Act contained standard directions: 'the right of common to be extinguished' and the land 'ploughed up, broken up or converted to tillage'. If this did not happen and the land was subsequently not cultivated then a fine of £5 per acre would be enforced. If cattle were allowed to roam onto inclosed land, they could be impounded and a fine of '5s per animal' would be levied. The locals were really going to have to get on with it and give up their old ways. Gates and fences had to be erected but no trees or shrubs were to be destroyed unless the owners agreed. Leasing was to be permitted but not to 'a minor, an idiot, lunatic, or a person beyond the seas'. The Act was about to enforce a massive change to the life of the town.

The eight commissioners, who were paid to enforce the Act, were sworn in at a meeting held on 13th April 1774 and there followed a flurry of meetings, held at the White Lion Inn. The meetings were recorded by Mr William Hunt, the Town Clerk, and the document that resulted gives a rare insight into how such a great change was organised. There was to be no further delay - after the swearing in of the commissioners, a second meeting was called for 9am the next day. At this second meeting the landowners were instructed to 'mark their land' by the next meeting set for the 25th April, ten days later. Territory was marked out with stakes at appropriate places and once an area was confirmed as accurate, the stakes would be driven well into the ground. At that point it was illegal to remove them. If a landowner failed to take this action, their land would be 'considered as common land'. That threat must have put paid to any thought of non-cooperation or foot-dragging by those less enamoured of the whole business.

The next four meetings, held between the 25th and 28th April, focussed on 'qualitifying the land' and on the 29th the landowners were instructed to specify the numbers of 'yard land, the odd lands, their proportions of meadow ground and the number of their horses, cows and sheep commons respectively' by the 12th May. A document, entitled the 'State of Property of Stratford and Welcomb intended to be enclosed' drawn up earlier in January 1774, revealed that Mr Keen had property made up of '4 yard lands and 4 lands without common, 8 cow commons, 8 horse commons, and 128 sheep commons' with rental income set at £66 10s 0d.[7] A yard land at this time could be anything between fifteen and forty acres. In nearby Warwick a yard land was considered to be thirty acres and that figure may well have applied here. In the calculations the cows, sheep and horses commons had differing value with ten sheep being equal to one cow common. When they had done so, if their claim was within Old Stratford, it was to be posted on Holy Trinity Church door for all to see. They were given twelve days to do so. A further meeting was arranged in the White Lion Inn for the '13th day of June' at which landowners were 'to say where they want their new fields to be within the common land' and if they wish to 'make any exchanges of lands'. These 'exchanges' allowed the landowners to swap parcels of land with each other.

A surveyor was appointed and at the 13th June meeting he was instructed to produce a plan to show 'quantities and qualities and values vested in the lands surveyed' along with the proposed roads. He only had until the 25th July to complete this task, but then everything came to a complete standstill when it was revealed that two important roads were to be 'stopped up'. They were Back Lane (Grove Road) and Pound Lane (Arden Street, *see* Fig 1). As both marked the northern edge of town, this was vigorously opposed. Independent opinion was called for. The commissioners were invited to think again, which they did, and both roads were saved.

If closed roads were contentious issues, so too was the right to allow horses to graze on the roadside. There had been nothing especially contentious about this when there were no fences and the roadside grass offered a free supply of pasture, but now this right had to be more clearly defined. It was permissible to graze on 'the grass and herbage growing and renewing in and upon all and every road and highway' but not on the turnpike roads to Henley, Alcester, Warwick and Evesham. This herbage was reserved for the respective lords of the manors.

At the next meeting, on 13th June, any disagreement amongst the landowners was probably resolved or was well on the way to being so. Now they had to appear in person at the White Lion Inn with their petitions stating the 'situation of their respective allotments'. Mr Keen's petition carefully described where he wanted his new land (Fig 5).

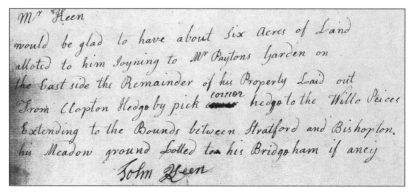

Fig 5. John Keen makes his request c.1775

At some point following the 13thJune meeting, the commissioners finalised matters. Keen was allotted land 'in lieu of full compensation' and he had 'all that plot of land containing 83 acres 1 rod 37 perches'.[8] He also received a further '3 acres 3 rods 9 perches near Clopton Bridge'. In total he received eighty-six acres, five rods and six perches exactly where he wanted. The Mayfield Avenue land had finally gained a new owner. Moreover, some of Mr Keen's land sat alongside that of Mr Payton. They were close neighbours living in Henley Street and clearly also good friends. It is therefore worth noting that Mr Payton's request was also granted: that his new land be in 'the Guild Pitts quarter 'opposite the back end of my house I dwell in and extending eastwards and north to the Warwick Road'. If both men looked eastwards out of their back windows *all* the visible countryside was about to become theirs.

Throughout 1775, meetings continued and exchanges, costs and rights of way were discussed. On the 24th September it was declared that all activity was to cease and 'all must be extinguished by the 25th Day of October'. The land had been allotted to 'twenty persons'. At that point a very relieved Mr Hunt, the Town Clerk, put down his pen having completed his record.

During all the meetings the final cost must have been on everyone's minds. When the final figure of £1,407 15s 1½d was announced it would have come as quite a shock. This total, the result of meticulous book keeping, was double the earlier estimated cost of £740 stated by Mr Smith and Mr Ashwin back in 1773. On the 3rd December 'A Notice of Expenses' was posted on the church door and the landowners had little option but to pay up. Mr Keen's expenses came to £99 3s 4 ½d and his claim was 'enrolled' (made legal) on 3rd October 1775.[9] From that date he had four calendar months to put up his fences and install any gates necessary for 'free access along footpaths'. The landowners had to toe the line when it came to the cost. If they failed to pay up, their goods and chattels could be seized, although they could appeal to the Quarter Session 'if persons shall think... themselves aggrieved'.

If the new land owners were shocked at the final cost, they could at least console themselves with the thought of future increased crops and profit; the dispossessed poor had no such consolation. Nationally their discontent became widespread and in a later act, the General Enclosure Act of 1845, it was required that land be set aside as 'field garden' for the poor and in this way allotments were made available for the deserving poor. This idea, raised much earlier, had been disregarded by the landowners who did not want to relinquish acres of their land. Their resistance was only overcome when it became clear that in offering allotments, the Poor Rate (a tax to support the destitute) could be seriously reduced. However back in Stratford in 1775 there was no such requirement in law and there appears to have been no land set aside for the local poor - and this despite it being generally understood that a labourer usually earned a wage insufficient to support his family and relied on the common land to survive. It was a hard time for the poor in Stratford and many left town to seek a different, and hopefully better, life in nearby Birmingham.

If there was no land reserved for the poor to cultivate, it was at least proposed that land be 'set out' for a hospital for them, to be managed by the church wardens. The location of this hospital was defined in general terms and involved the Alcester Road but, once again, the poor lost out - this did not happen until 109 years later when a philanthropic family stepped in.

The changes imposed with inclosure were drastic and irreversible. Relationships among the wealthy had been tested and strained; some no doubt were never to recover. Mr Keen had a little over twelve more years to live and become accustomed to his new situation. Did he take pleasure in the fact that he could now stroll from the back of his house on Henley Street, across Gill Pitts (Guild Street), up the hill, across a footpath and down to the river and it was entirely across his own fields? For the first time he could view his land as a whole and this must have had a powerful influence on his future actions; he had a substantial number of acres further to the north, extending towards Bishopton, but this land was on his doorstep.

He was about to lose his only son and heir which would cause him and his wife, Mary, grief. With this loss he would also lose the secure future he had expected for his land. His son's death was an event that he no doubt placed firmly in the hands of God, in divine providence, something beyond his control, but he could control the future of his property. He called in a lawyer and wrote a complex will; his land was to have protection in an uncertain future.

Chapter 2

The White Lion Inn

Throughout the troubled years, when inclosure was a hot topic, the White Lion on Henley Street (Fig 2 No. 34) was *the* place to hold important meetings. As importantly, it's owner Mr John Payton was instrumental (albeit somewhat accidentally) in promoting Shakespeare's reputation when he energetically supported the first lavish event celebrating Shakespeare's name. As a result of his exertions the White Lion Inn gained a national reputation and the scene was set for the remarkable change that was to engulf Stratford. As such it has earned the right to its own dedicated chapter.

Mr Payton became the proprietor of the Swan Inn on Henley Street when he bought the premises from the Rev Thomas Horne in 1746. In 1751 he expanded his business further when he bought the freehold of the White Lion. Recognising the important potential of the site he went on to buy adjoining land from a certain Shakespeare Hart and rented even more from Stratford Corporation. He became the owner of an establishment of impressive size, placed in what he considered to be a prime location.

In 1753 he began an extravagant programme to, effectively, rebuild the entire inn, for which he paid a builder £825. He demanded that the main gateway be thirty feet wide and that the main building extend three stories high. With its impressive façade and impressive dimensions it was a remarkable change for humble Henley Street. Using brick for his grand design, he was following a fashion that was soon to be followed all around Stratford. Many timber-framed houses were subsequently faced with brick, the timber being revealed many years later when fashions changed yet again.

Unlike his main competitors, the Falcon Inn on Chapel Street and the Shakespeare Hotel in High Street, Mr Payton was not constrained by narrow courts, alleyways and roads. As the facilities on offer at the White Lion became more extravagant he was compelled to rent even more Henley Street land from the Corporation. His successful application for nearby land under the inclosure legislation ensured that further, and more innovative, expansion was possible. Not content with making the buildings impressive he also set about making the grounds into an attraction. Over time he provided a pleasure garden, a melon garden, a bowling green and a famous Mulberry tree that apparently had Shakespearean connections. These entertainments were situated to the east and across Guild Pitts. Horses and carriages arriving from London and Birmingham would enter the impressive courtyard, making this an increasingly busy side of town (Fig 6).

Fig 6 Sketch of the White Lion back gateway, completed in the late 1700's

Later he catered for the needs of the local hunting fraternity by providing kennels which was quite a ground-breaking thing to do at the time. By developing the inn as he did, he cleverly maintained a varied clientele, ranging from the rumbustious local sporty set to more refined visitors from further afield. As an indication of its status, on the 1759 plan, his was the only inn to be named (Fig 7 listed as 26).

By extending the grounds he had set the course for creating one of the most famous inns in England.

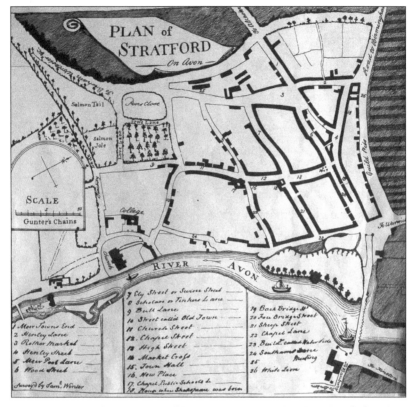

Fig 7 Plan of Stratford by Samuel Winter showing the White Lion Inn (26) 1759

The White Lion continued to go from strength to strength and the 1765 smallpox census records thirty-nine people as living there (only two had *not* had the pox).[10] They would have included kitchen maids, cooks, waiters, porters, grooms, gardeners, ostlers, boot boys and chambermaids as well as the paying guests. It would not have been a bad life; at the time the inn was described as a place that 'buzzed' with activity. Depending on what one reads, it seems that Payton was either greatly admired or hugely disliked. He was described, by some, as arrogant and rude and the service he provided as condescending; others could not praise him, and the inn, enough.

The Garrick Jubilee

The grand Garrick Jubilee of 1769 came about largely because of Mr Payton's enthusiasm. Three days of elaborate celebrations were set to mark the official opening of the new Town Hall, which had been paid for by Mr Payton, and the unveiling of a bust of Shakespeare. It also coincidentally marked two hundred years (more or less) since the birth of Shakespeare. It was effectively this event that kicked off Stratford as a place of pilgrimage, 'Bardolatory' had been born and the 'future of the Borough stems from Garrick's decision to hold his jubilee here'. This despite the event being a washout due to torrential rain and there being 'no Shakespeare words in the whole event'.[11]

Payton was determined that his inn would attract the most visitors, and to this end he enlarged the inn by adding a large assembly room, a card room, a coffee room and a small suite of private apartments for the famous actor Mr David Garrick and his wife. From London he ordered 'three hundred dozen pewter plates, the same of pewter spoons and knives and forks and fifty dozen stewpans and kettles,' this in addition to hundreds of sedan chairs brought in from Bath and London. The table service was faultless and three hundred additional waiters were employed from the capital (the numbers involved, published in a contemporary public ledger, may well have been inflated). It says something about human nature that, even after this effort and expenditure, some guests were unimpressed and felt that his monopoly on hospitality 'rendered the over-bearing keeper additionally presuming' – and if the poor pampered guest complained, that had no effect because to do so caused the waiters 'to ignore you'.

The end result of the Garrick Jubilee was that Payton made a loss, and not a small one. In his enthusiasm and ambition, he over-extended and in 1770 was forced to borrow £1,000 from the Lucy family at Charlecote. In 1778 he was compelled to borrow even more money simply to stay in business. In 1779 he housed the new post office and it was possibly to raise additional income from residents lingering for the arrival of the Royal Mail coach. He died in 1780 without writing a will, and it was left to Ann his widow to deal with his estate. In

January of the following year, she renounced the administration of his affairs and his only son and heir had to sort out the financial mess.

Mr John Payton junior was in his early thirties when he inherited the inn and, from the start, he lacked his father's ambition and enthusiasm for the business. He passed the daily running of the inn to resident landlords whilst he lived elsewhere. His interest focused on civic duty. He was elected an alderman in 1780 and was mayor in 1795 and 1801. His interest may have appeared to focus on civic duty but he was not always so keen to turn up to the Borough meetings. He was not alone in this. In 1788 non–attendance of aldermen at meetings was so bad that Borough business could not be conducted. Fines were introduced that year to encourage attendance and Payton was promptly fined five shillings.[12] In 1790 he was fined again, on that occasion for leaving a meeting early.

Mr Payton junior walked away from the inn but he could not ignore its financial problems. Six years after the death of his father confidence in him had completely ebbed away and in 1786 his debts were called in. Despite successfully resisting bankruptcy he later, in 1790, put his estate in trust to be sold. After this attempt to sell failed, any interest he had in the White Lion must surely have reached a low ebb but he struggled on. Two years after the death of his wife in 1802 he wrote his will and made clear that he had no desire to pass the business to his son, another John.

Although a visit in 1806 of George IV, then the Prince Regent, may have temporarily lifted his spirits, in 1811 he again attempted to sell. This time the inn and grounds were split into individual Lots for auction. There were four Lots in total, the White Lion Inn being Lot 1. It was described as a 'long established and highly respectable inn' but it failed to find a buyer and the reserve price of £8,250 was not met. Times were indeed hard. Mr Payton was still the reluctant owner when he died on the 3rd July 1818, leaving his son John to sell the inn 'for the best price'.

It was not until 1822 that two brothers, Thomas and James Arkell, paid £4,400 for the inn. Ominously they took out a £3,000 loan to do so. Although Thomas Arkell had at one time briefly managed the inn, the two Arkell brothers appear to have been blinded by its former reputation and did not see the true situation - that its best days were over. Perhaps they thought they could do better: Stratford had as many as twenty-four passenger coaches arriving and departing every day, many from the inn, and it must certainly have appeared as busy as ever. In truth, ever since those grand celebrations of 1769 the inn had become something of a millstone to the owners and from 1822 it was more of a curse.

Appearances were deceptive: in 1830 there was a visit of the Duchess of Kent with the twelve-year-old Princess Victoria and there were the inevitable Bard's birthday celebrations but by the end of that year, and just eight years after buying the inn, it all started to go very wrong. Thomas Arkell died in December followed by his wife, seventeen days later. This left their nineteen-year-old son and heir, Thomas, with a desperate legal fight on his hands. The court finally ruled, in 1832, that all was to be made over to his uncle James 'in trust' to be sold, debts to be paid off, and any residual money to be shared between *all* the children. Small plots of land were sold off and the inn went to auction in 1834. But James Arkell's efforts failed and he was made a bankrupt and promptly died. Subsequently, Ann, his widow, had to arrange yet another auction and in 1836 the inn and land was sold to Mr John Warden, a coal dealer. This was a speculative venture and Warden set up another auction in 1838 when the once spectacular pleasure-gardens were divided into nineteen yet smaller lots. This was to appeal to property developers and the Mulberry Street residential area came into being. The inn ceased trading sometime in 1860 and one year later Warden went bankrupt - and died very soon after.

Nearly all trace of the White Lion building was lost when it was bulldozed in 1979 at the instigation of the Birthplace Trust to make way for their Shakespeare Centre.

Chapter 3

Mr Keen & Henley Street

Mr John Keen was a wealthy man and made a good living as a maltster, germinating barley in order to increase the sugars in the grain and thus produce the malt that is needed in the brewing process. A constant supply of beer was essential because people literally drank it like water - the local water supply could at times become contaminated. Fortunately the Stratford area offered the correct conditions for a good brew and from the 16th to the 19th century malting was the town's principle industry. There were, at various times, malt houses in all the main streets in Stratford. They were so numerous that early in the 17th century there was unrest as a consequence. So much grain was being used for malting at a time when food was in short supply that in 1630 restrictions were put in place that released more grain for food.

In 1775, Mr Keen was about sixty years old and he still had fifteen more years to live. He was born around 1714 and grew up in nearby Harbury. He married his first wife, Elizabeth Bruce in 1735 and together they had Elizabeth, Joseph and Mary. Sadly Elizabeth died aged just eleven. When John's wife died in 1758 he married Mary Jones that same year and she was to become his 'dear wife Mary'. Keen, the successful business man, was also a religious man and in 1761, along with fourteen other men, he acted as trustee in buying a 'meeting house, or place for public and religious worship by the Congregation of Protestant Dissenters'. This meeting house was on Rother Street and later became the United Reformed Church, still there today. The other men concerned also ran profitable local businesses: a button maker, a hatter, a joiner, a grocer, two ironmongers, a linen draper, a silversmith, a tanner, an innkeeper, two flax dressers and also two 'gentlemen'.

It would have been a great sadness to Keen when, in December 1786, his only son, Joseph, died. Until Joseph's death, he had intended his estate to pass to Joseph and then to Joseph's son (Joseph had one daughter at the time). Mary, Keens' surviving daughter, was married and living elsewhere. Mr Keen was only too well aware that on inheriting his land Mary would in reality be passing it to her husband, his son-in-law, the Reverend Joel Morris. The law at the time did not allow women to own property in their own right on marriage. The couple had just had their ninth child and certainly were not short of sons. Mr Keen, rightly or wrongly, was concerned that his land would be sold off in a piece-meal fashion to provide an income for their large family. With this disturbing thought, and just three months after the death of Joseph, he set about ensuring that he held considerable sway over the future of his land when he was dead and buried. He did this by writing a restrictive will (*see* Chapter 5).

17 Henley Street

The site of Mr Keen's home has an interesting history with a Shakespearean connection. Shakespeare's father had used the rooms to the right of his premises as storage space but for many years thereafter they became an inn variously known as the Swan, the Maidenhead and finally, in the 1850's, the Swan and Maidenhead Inn. The house that Keen had lived and died in, known earlier as the Bell, was situated next to this inn and later became 17 Henley Street. He bought it in 1756 or some short time after from a Mrs Norcliffe.

Today you can stand in Henley Street and see exactly where Mr Keen lived. Unfortunately, it is the fire-break to the right of the famous 'Birthplace'. The house he occupied was inherited by his numerous grandchildren who, as we shall learn, were very eager to realise their inheritance. They had sold it in 1808 to Mr George Barke for £350, whose ownership was short and unhappy and involved demolition, rebuilding and bankruptcy. To conclude a long story, the house was sold in 1856 for £1,000 to the Birthplace Trustees who knocked it down.

Mr Keen also owned the houses next door, numbers 15 and 16, often referred to as 'Hornebyes cottages'. He had acquired them in 1760 from the same Mrs Norcliffe from whom he acquired number 17 and he may have briefly lived in one or both of them. When walking into the Shakespeare Birthplace Gift Shop you are in Mr Keen's property and as close to him as you can possibly get. He sold this property in 1782 to Mr John Warren for £130. It was therefore absent from his will and beyond the reach of his acquisitive grandchildren.

Fig 8. Sketch showing properties on Henley Street (undated)

Figure 8 shows a sketch of the famous birth place *c.*1850 divided into two, Shakespeare's home being the black and white timbered section. The right half bricked over, being then the Swan and Maidenhead Inn. Next to that is Mr Barke's fine house built on the site of the Bell Inn where Keen had lived. This impressive house is the one demolished to form the firebreak to the right. Butting up to this house is Keen's second small property, now the gift shop.

In the mid 1800's, photographs were taken of the Birthplace and in them we can follow the fate of Mr Keen's plot, tight up against the right side of the Shakespeare property. Figure 9 shows the complete demolition of the property to the left of the famous house thereby revealing its rough structure.

Fig 9. Firebreak to the left of the famous building created c.1856

Fig 10. Firebreaks in place c.1885

Figure 10 shows the work completed and the building made safe from fire on both sides, and altered almost beyond recognition. Keen's two remaining cottages, to the right, have yet to be converted into the gift shop

Stratford's position on the River Avon meant that the wealth and well-being of its residents was very much linked to the ups and downs of the river's navigational status. As early as 1639 it was open to trade from Bristol and the town subsequently thrived but in 1775, when Keen was negotiating for his new land, both the river and town were in a period of decline caused by 'a falling off in the Avon navigation'. It was reported in 1781 that one in ten houses in the town were unoccupied. Things improve gradually with the passing of various turnpike acts that improved the roads, encouraging the arrival of mail coaches and visitors. Mr Keen's friend, Mr John Payton, owner of the White Lion Inn, was pivotal in these new developments. When, in 1816 the canal opened, linking Birmingham and Bristol, the Bancroft basin became a busy industrial site with coal wharves, timber yards and dry docks.

Mr Keen did not live to see these improvements and, although the town was in decline during his lifetime, the Keen's family life was comfortable. There was property and land and a son to inherit; his daughter Mary was happily married with children; there was much to celebrate and life was reasonably safe. The threat of highway robbery was diminishing with the new roads, and night-watchmen patrolled the streets to ensure safety after dark. Unfortunately, there was very little in the form of healthcare and it came at a price. Smallpox immunisation was available, although it was still a rather a hit-and-miss affair. Apothecaries could be called upon for herbal remedies. If the patient was rich, as Mr Keen was, he could take himself off to a fashionable spa, possibly to nearby Leamington, to drink the waters. Mr Charles Pestell, living on Rother Street Market, was the local surgeon and may well have treated the Keens. Most interventions were painful since anaesthesia was in its infancy and, needless to say, treatments associated with teeth were little short of barbaric.

But on a deeper level life was not so comfortable. The king was about to have his first debilitating attack of porphyria, which would be interpreted as madness. The industrialised cities were rapidly expanding and their factories were churning out cheap goods. The rich were getting richer but the plight of the poor was getting worse. The price of bread had risen alarmingly and was hitting the poorest the hardest. The Government's response to the simmering unrest and riot was to increase the number of crimes punishable by death. These were troubling times for Mr Keen and his fellow landowners as they sat in the White Lion Inn

Chapter 4

Insurrection

Until the end of the eighteenth century, when much of the country was rocked by outbursts of rioting, Stratford remained a relatively peaceful place. One recorded riot occurred back in 1619 and was caused by the appearance of a Maypole. But gradually as the nineteenth century unfolded Stratford residents increasingly took to the streets. Often it came about because of deep political differences but unrest could also flair up over religious divisions. The eminent men who sat in the White Lion discussing the state of the nation were often also the Justices of the Peace (JPs) responsible for dishing out punishment and keeping the peace. JPs dealt with a wide range of offences either at the Stratford Petty Sessions or at the Quarter Sessions. The Quarter Sessions were conducted by at least two JPs with a judge in attendance and met quarterly, at Epiphany, Lent, Midsummer and Michaelmas. The Petty Sessions, less formal affairs often held in the Falcon Inn on Fridays, had come about because there was too much work for the Quarter Sessions. The frequency of the Petty Session meetings was therefore determined by the level of crime in the area. More serious crimes were referred to the Assize Court in Warwick where lengthy imprisonment, transportation or the death penalty were increasingly the outcome.

In 1792, just two years after the death of Mr Keen, a large group of worried local magistrates and gentlemen of Warwickshire met in the White Lion Inn. The French Revolution was well under way and its influence was seen as a threat. They intended to uphold George III's recent instruction to 'enforce the late Proclamation issued by His Majesty against Seditious and Republican Libells', the product of 'ill-disposed persons of his Kingdom in Conjunction with Foreign Emissaries'.[13] The magistrates and gentlemen of Warwickshire wanted to preserve 'public tranquillity' and were aware that 'Seditious publications' were exciting 'the lower classes'. The discontent and mayhem among the lower orders appeared to be the product of public meetings which were often held in local inns; they decided to withdraw the licence of any publican who allowed such meetings on his premises.

Their edict did not improve the situation. In 1800 the Mayor, Richard Allen, offered a huge reward for information leading to the arrest of perpetrators of the 'shameful riots and disturbances' although whether this resulted in a conviction is not known. There was however a conviction two years later, in 1802, when Mr Izod, on behalf of the Borough, presented a £21 reward to Joseph Miles for information leading to the 'conviction of William Sambridge at the last Assizes'. Although the French Revolution and the Irish Rebellion were over, revolution was still in the air provoking the fear that minor disturbances might ignite into full-scale riot.

Not all the mayhem was directly due to political grievance. In January of 1806, George Whitehead, Richard Cleaver, his wife Mary, and twenty other people were brought before a local jury for causing 'great scandal and disgrace of public morals and Religion' in Southam; it was not exactly a riot, being more of an angry gathering, but it was enough to get the already jumpy authorities to act.[14] The indictment stated that they caused 'a very great terror, disturbance and grievance' to 'many of his majesty's quiet and peaceable subjects' who were 'passing about their lawful affairs and business'. Richard Cleaver had tied a 'halter and cord about the waist' of his wife and 'in the public market place...unlawfully, scandalously and immorally did exhibit Mary Cleaver'. He did so for half an hour or upwards before he 'did deliver her over to George Whitehead'. At the time this was a generally accepted way for the poor to obtain a recognised separation. But the additional twenty people involved, 'were making great noises' for over an hour. It was clearly an unpleasant business but hardly seditious. Everyone involved was rounded up and charged.

Fear of the mob did not diminish and, perhaps with reason, public gatherings were seriously discouraged. Three years later, in 1809, Francis Lowe and forty others were brought before the court because, on April the 10[th,] 'with force of arms unlawfully, riotously, riotously and tumultuously they did assemble and gather together'.[15] Their purpose was to have Joseph Kettle and William Taylor 'fight and combat with force and violence'. It was another unpleasant event and probably involved betting, but it was not seditious. Once again, everyone was arrested.

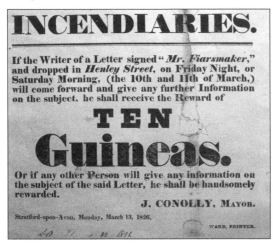

Fig 11 Poster offering the reward for Mr Fiarsmaker 1826

Matters became more serious when, in 1826, the Mayor, Dr Connolly, called a meeting in the Town Hall (Fig 2 No. 9) on the 11th March to address an outbreak of arson on local farms. The destruction had been 'trifling so far' and no theft was involved but he viewed each outbreak with horror. The meeting agreed to encourage subscriptions for a reward leading to conviction. There was already a poster up in town offering a reward of fifty guineas. Things moved more rapidly than expected. A letter had been dropped in Henley Street, signed 'Mr Fiarsmaker'. A very prompt reward of ten guineas was offered on the 13th March (Fig 11). By the 20th March a new poster went up. Not only had Dr Connolly and his committee gathered £300, a truly huge amount of money, but other interested parties had joined in. The King, via Robert Peel the Home Secretary, offered a pardon to anyone involved willing to inform.

Two years later in, 1828, the Mayor, John Higgins, was so alarmed at potential unrest that he called a public meeting, this time in the Falcon Inn, to consider how recurring outbreaks of arson could be stopped. Arson attacks were widespread, particularly in counties to the south, and known as the 'Swing Riots'. They were protests against rural poverty, barns and hayricks being the usual targets. The population of the country had increased by 50%, in less than thirty years and it did not help that the crops of 1828 and 1829 were poor. Stratford's population had increased by 44% but it was still sufficient to cause unrest. Arson attacks in the Stratford area continued well into 1829 with five fires in the first two months of that year prompting the County Fire Officer to offer a further reward of £200.

The local arsonist was not caught and events did not spiral into widespread public disorder as feared. It is interesting to note the sentences passed at the time. Following a trial at the Warwick Midsummer Session, three prisoners all received seven years transportation, one for stealing a handkerchief, another for stealing a table cloth and the third for stealing a mat, while a fourth was whipped and discharged for stealing a cheese. If Stratford's arsonist had been arrested he would have been hanged, this being the usual punishment for arson.

The 1832 Stratford riot

If the countryside expressed unrest with outbursts of arson, the town of Stratford chose riot. It started with the usual rumbustious behaviour commonly associated with local elections. When the 1831 Reform Bill failed 590 Stratford residents felt sufficiently aggrieved to send a petition to London on 2nd October. Nearby Birmingham and other large cities rioted. The 1832 the Great Reform Act was seen by the Prime Minister, Earl Grey, as a prompt, pragmatic response and a reasonable measure 'to prevent the necessity of revolution'. Nevertheless there had been 'great disappointment' at the 1832 Act. In England and Wales only approximately 217,000 voters were added to the existing 435,000, this among a population of over fourteen million. The Act included a £10 property requirement that effectively excluded most working class men. As a result bad feelings were still running high in town. An election offered the opportunity to express them.

It began on the first day of the election on the 17th December. The unrest centred on the White Lion Inn on Henley Street, run by Martha Ridler and her son Charles and a polling place. It was also where 'Mr Shirley's committee sat' (Mr Evelyn John Shirley) which was 'for the orange colour, the blues being elsewhere'(Sir Gray Skipwith and Sir George Philips). The two colours denoted the two political parties involved. There was a 'sort of gradual confusion in the town and a mob assembled at various points' - according to Constable William Goodwin who 'lost his hat and got his shins kicked' when he tried to disband the men. Later the 'confusion' became a riot that spread round town, the mob smashing windows and assaulting the two other available constables, Ashfield and Keeley. By 2 pm the constables were facing a crowd of three hundred in Ely Street which by 4 pm it had grown to between four and five hundred and had moved to the White Lion Inn. The ringleaders carried 'bludgeons and weapons' as well as stones.

Late that afternoon, the Riot Act was read, which gave the local magistrates the power to summon help if there were more than twelve people 'unlawfully assembled exhibiting tumult and riotous behaviour'.[16] The militia were sent for from Coventry which would have alarmed the rioters; the Manchester riot, dubbed the 'Peterloo Massacre', just fourteen years before had not been forgotten. Little wonder that their arrival in town was greatly feared and everyone went home. By 10 pm, when the soldiers eventually arrived, all was quiet. The next day, 18th December, special constables were drafted in because the JP's were of the opinion 'that the ordinary officers appointed for preserving the Peace are not sufficient to the preservation of Peace'. There were still two more days of polling to get through.

Eight men, thought to be the ring leaders, were recognised by Constable John Ashfield and others were named by members of the public. They were brought before the magistrates at the Christmas session of the Quarter Sessions in Warwick.[17] George Gibbins was considered the worst because he said he 'didn't care for any of the bloody constables'. Another ring leader was George Cope. Sarah

Reason, who at the time was living in Windsor Street, said she saw Cope leaving 'Becket's with a poker', saying 'damn my eyes if I don't murder somebody with this before I have done with it'. Later in the evening when he encountered Constable Keeley he threatened to 'split his skull open'. Twelve people were eventually sent to gaol for rioting. The opinion of the magistrates was that the riot had nothing to do with the election. The men 'just fancied it was a good opportunity for them to shew off' and there was no intention to 'prevent people casting their vote'. Along with the punishment that was meted out to the prisoners there were expressions of sympathy for the lives of the out-of-work poor and for Mr Charles Ridler who had to pay £20 to 'repair the injury done' to the White Lion Inn.

After this troubled interlude there was very little unrest during the troubled 1840s and the local JPs had to wait until 1860 before they dealt with an enthusiastic preacher called John Wallace who created sufficient havoc that it might be described as a riot. He was brought before the Petty Sessions for 'obstructing the free passage'. He denied this and maintained he was preaching not obstructing. The rowdy crowd who were trying to prevent him was estimated to be between 800 and 2,000. The JP disagreed with the preacher and fined him £1 with 16s costs. This religious intolerance and division was to surface again in the 1880s when two religious groups were in fierce competition, not only with each other but also with the government, over control of the town's schools.

Strike action

Serious dissatisfaction resurfaced in 1877 and took the form of a strike. The rising middle classes were experiencing good times and were having lavish villas built, particularly to the east in New Town Ward. The bricklayers were paid 7d per hour, which gave a weekly wage of 33s. In the summer of 1877 they asked for a ½d per hour raise but were refused by the masters who considered that 'it was fair remuneration for value received' especially as the hours were so good (home at 5.30 each day and on Saturday by 1.30). But, argued the workers, the present rate of 7d was misleading because they were stood off during bad weather which had the effect of reducing the rate to 5d per hour and since business was booming the increase could be afforded. The progress of this stand-off was reported weekly in the local paper, the *Herald*.[18] Forty workers, members of the Stratford branch of the Operative Bricklayers Society, went on strike and were paid 12s per week from the Society funds. Meanwhile a few of the workers had gone to Birmingham where they were paid 9d per hour and others went to Leamington and were paid 7½d. Three weeks into the strike the masters remained firm and were recruiting replacement workers. If the men wanted their jobs back then it was to be 'on old terms'. The *Herald* reported that the men and their families were suffering. Six weeks from its start the strike came to a sudden end after the masters at last offered the ½d extra. They had apparently experienced pressure from clients who wanted them to get on with their smart new houses. For the low paid workers, and there were very many in Stratford with its agricultural background, life remained hard and requests, published in the *Herald* in 1886, for donations of 'beef dripping, money and cake' for the ½d breakfasts for poor children, are testament to this.

The 1900 riot

Over sixty years after the 1832 election riot, Stratford experienced riot again. The Boer Wars of 1880-1881 and 1899-1902 were the most expensive wars waged to that date and were seen by many, especially the Liberals in town, as inappropriate colonial intervention. Opposition to the wars was heightened by news of the deaths in 'concentration camps' of women and children which, it was felt, brought shame on the nation. In 1899 opinions in Stratford were, as ever, so divided that it didn't take much to set off riotous behaviour. Stratford had just four constables at the time and there were at least five scenes of unrest in town. In the initial confusion, the Riot Act was not read out in good time and so the militia were not summoned for help until a lot of damage had been done. This compromised the compensation on offer for broken windows. One shop owner could only claim a measly one penny per pebble collected in his shop; people were not happy.

During the celebrations in town marking the relief of the siege of Ladysmith Mr Henry Bullard, a congregationalist, had apparently 'made himself obnoxious' by expressing his anti-war opinions. This was when protecting his antique shop on Chapel street from an attack.[19] Mr Bullard was a brave man to do this as the crowd, led by a Mr James Marr, was approximately three-hundred strong. As the crowd left the scene one rioter shouted 'don't listen to his soft soap'. This was after causing considerable damage. The crowd reassembled the following day and the very angry Mr Marr and his men shattered 166 panes of glass, thereby wrecking Mr Bullard's auction rooms on Guild Street (Fig 2 No. 23). Surprisingly at the Warwick hearing only three ring leaders were imprisoned, each for a month, whilst the fourth had his charge reduced from riot to drunk and disorderly. Even more surprisingly, at a separate hearing in Stratford the jury was asked to decide whether an old lady passing by would have feared for her life; if yes then it was riot. The jury could not agree and so after an hour the prisoner was discharged with a 'there's an end to it'.

When more trouble surfaced in 1910 the cause was an unpopular budget. Dubbed 'The people's budget' it was brought in by David Lloyd George, the Chancellor of the Exchequer, assisted by Winston Churchill at the Board of Trade, known at the time as the 'terrible twins'. Their aim was to raise money to pay for social welfare programmes intended to put paid to the poverty that, both men thought, blighted society. It was a budget to redistribute wealth and there was nothing in it to demonstrate against. However, included in the budget was a land tax that caused considerable consternation. Land taxes had been around for very many years but possibly, the new land tax was purposely misrepresented by its opponents.

At any rate, the demonstrators in Fig 12 seem to have thought their bread was about to be taxed when quite the opposite was true. To get the 'People's Budget' passed, the land tax was dropped. The men must have felt that their posturing had been effective.

Fig 12 A protest at a possible new tax on bread 1910

'The Great Unrest'

'The Great Unrest' lasted from 1911 to 1914 and began with a miners' strike. Its significance, in labour relations, was said to be as great as that of the later General Strike of 1926 but it was far less reported. Waves of unofficial strikes shook the political establishment, 872 occurring in 1911 alone. The workforce who had been the mainstay of the preceding period of industrial growth was now not so compliant. As Lenin was to say later: 'The workers have learnt to fight'.

In April Mr George Boyden, the editor of the *Herald*, expressed relief that the national coal strike was at an end, although he added that an increase in the cost of living, not being matched by a similar rise in wages, was wrong. He had, in an earlier edition, questioned whether it 'was worth the price which has been paid'. By 1914 'The Great Unrest' was coming to an end, prompted by the outbreak of the First World War, although Stratford witnessed a final demonstration that year (Fig 13). There was however still plenty of unruly behaviour and it was associated with the issue of women's suffrage. This is dealt with in Chapter 20.

The period of 'The Great Unrest' did not evolve into a revolution possibly because of a slew of changes instigated by the Liberals, beginning with free school meals in 1906; two years later came pensions for those aged over seventy years; Labour Exchanges appeared in 1909; in the same year the notorious back-to-back housing was outlawed; in 1911 the National Insurance Act provided insurance cover for workers and the opportunity to see a GP, which in turn paved the way for the National Health Service of 1948. These reforms gave only basic protection but they highlight how dire life was before.

JPs were well aware of the hard lives of the labourers who came before them and would, on occasion, use their discretion. If this occasional mildness was repeated across the country, it, along with legislative improvement, may also have helped the country avoid revolution.

Fig 13 Stratford workers demonstrate 1914

Mr Albert Danks

An example of this occasional mildness was reported in the *Herald* in 1912 and concerned Mr Albert Danks and his duck. The case concerned the receiving of a stolen duck. Danks, a fish-hook maker by trade, was accused of receiving a duck worth five shillings, for which he paid one shilling, from Harry Clayton and George Thatcher. He gave a very long explanation about how he came by the duck, what he thought about the duck, and his complete and utter surprise to discover that, in fact, the duck was stolen. He therefore pleaded not guilty. The bench retired for a short time. On their return the chairman said to Albert 'you have done a foolish thing'. He was however 'given the benefit of the doubt' and discharged. At this time 43-year-old Danks was living with his wife Lucy and their eight children. With ages ranging from three to nineteen there were a lot of mouths to feed. It would have been a hard life and the chance of a cheap duck could not be missed-and the JPs knew it to be so.

Chapter 5

Mr Keen's Will

Mr John Keen and his wife Mary lost their son Joseph in 1786, just eleven years after the Inclosure. Joseph, their only son, was set to inherit the land and, until Joseph's death, Keen could have faced his own death knowing that his wife Mary would be cared for and his land would remain intact. Joseph had married and had a daughter, Susannah, but now, with his death, everything had changed. All Mr Keen owned would, on his death, go to his daughter Mary and this was, in effect, handing his land to her husband, a Welsh Baptist Minister, the Reverend Joel Morris. The couple were living in Stretton-on-Fosse and at the time of Joseph's death had six surviving children, four sons and two daughters. Keen could well imagine the financial needs of such a large family and how his life's work could be regarded as a source of large amounts of cash. It would appear that Mr Keen was not happy with this situation. It may be that with the 1775 act of Inclosure and the subsequent consolidation of his scattered land he had acquired ideas above his station; to see his achievement destroyed by piecemeal auctioning instigated by his son-in-law was unacceptable.

There is recorded, in the United Reformed Church's papers, the death of a John Keen on 24th October 1790. Given his past commitment to that church, he is probably this John Keen. The early death of his only son in 1786 possibly prompted him to write his complicated will.[20] We know for sure that he made this will on the 10th March 1787 and that the will was proved 26th May 1791, pointing to a probable death in late 1790, which ties in with the United Reformed Church's records. Proving a will entailed making an inventory of all the dead person's possessions, presenting it, along with the will, to a church court which would agree that all was legal and it could therefore be acted upon – the granting of probate. In this instance, there was considerable delay to this final stage, not until the 2nd

34

October 1808, *eighteen years* after his death. This unusually long delay was due to a combination of events, the main one being that Mr Keen had arranged matters so that his son-in-law, could not readily sell up. His carefully constructed will was the means whereby he was able to control the future.

To his 'beloved wife Mary' he left his dwelling house and to 'have and use and enjoy all and singular my household goods and implements of household plate, china and furniture of all sorts'. However, should she 'not chuse to dwell in and occupy my said dwelling I revoke annul and make void the devises and bequests here in contained.' She would lose not only the house but an income secured by an annuity set up to give £30 per annum, to be paid 'half yearly on the 25th March and 29th September'. He stipulated that this bequest was conditional and that to qualify for it she must also 'release quit claim and give up her Dower or thirds at law which she might otherwise claim'. If she failed to agree to these conditions she would lose everything offered to her.

The right to dower

He was asking that his wife give up her right, in common law as a widow, to one third of all the land he had acquired during their marriage. This common-law right, known as 'thirds', gave some protection to wives who were, within the marriage, without property or income of their own. Even if their husbands tried to dispose of land via a detailed will, bequeathing land to others, the widow still retained her right to 'thirds'. This gave powerful protection to widows. Dower could cause obvious restrictions and complications to unhappily married husbands - or husbands concerned about their land, as was Mr Keen in this case. Some even made their brides 'bar' or give up this natural right before they said 'I do' at the altar. In the late 18th century, this was becoming an increasingly common practice. It was not good news for the women but was very good news for the solicitors who set up the complicated documentation required to create such a 'bar'. Keen, by writing this restriction into his will, gave his widow little option. She had been married to him for over thirty years and would have been entitled to a good inheritance under the rules of 'thirds'; however by accepting the conditions of the will she retained a home and an income even if she lost her right to dower. And the land remained intact – in theory.

The will stated that, upon her death, the house would go to his daughter Mary who would inherit his land for all 'her natural life' and thereafter to his son-in-law, Joel Morris, and thereafter to their sons and daughters who would be owners as 'tenants in common'. His land was situated down by the river where he owned Broad Meadow, Bridgham Square and Bridgham's Meadow, with more land extending up from Guild Pitts (Guild Street) and eastwards in Old Stratford (the land of this story). He also had extensive land extending from Clopton Street (Birmingham Road) towards Bishopton. As well as his land Mary was to get his 'large Bible'.

Mr Keen did not forget the progeny of his only son Joseph, who had predeceased him. Joseph's daughter, Susannah, had married John Hall and she would get the 'rent money' from property in Leicestershire. In this way she would be treated similarly to the other grandchildren. He thus side-stepped his daughter-in-law, Joseph's widow.

Mr Keen's will was proved by the Reverend Joel Morris on the 26th May 1791, in an ecclesiastic court as was the custom, but probate was not granted until the 2nd October 1808. The seventeen-year delay involved much wrangling and eventually recourse to the infamous Court of Chancery in London.

Chapter 6

Slavery

The year 1808 was set to be a momentous year for the Morris family. The previous year, 1807, had been even more momentous for the country, if after a rather different fashion. The Abolition of Slavery Act had finally been passed, and in Stratford the efforts of many locals had helped to bring it about.

Beginning in the late 18th and into the early 19th century abolitionists increased their efforts to stop not only the slave trade, but also the use of slave labour. From being the country that dominated the trade during the early 18th century, Britain rapidly reversed its attitude and began to lead the movement for abolition. Many Stratford residents signed the abolitionists' petitions, the Rev Thomas Leigh of nearby Adlestrop being much involved. He worked closely with Mr William Wilberforce and shared Wilberforce's passionate desire to end slavery.

As early as 1657 wealthy locals were expressing opposition to the slave trade but at this time they were very much in the minority. In subsequent years, Lord Thomas Leigh of Adlestrop, (an earlier relative of the Reverend Thomas Leigh mentioned above) along with the Duchess of Dudley, established a charitable trust to raise money for the local poor with an additional sum of £100 p.a. for the 'redemption of poor Christian slaves and captives from English slavery'.[21] By 1775 the trust intended £100 to be given to the 'East India Company and other 'companie' for this purpose. A letter of 1778 mentions figures totalling £700. Thirty-three years later, in 1811, the Reverend Thomas Leigh received a letter from Mr Thomas Hill Mortimer in London, who had presumably cast an objective eye over the accounts of the long-running trust, to the effect that the trust's money had not been going to rescue slaves but rather, it was suspected, to the local poor. There had been, at best, a 'want of application'. It was time, Hill suggested, to pursue the original aims of the charity. There was 'knowledge of a ship's crew in captivity who may probably be thought to be within the meaning of the charity', a timely move because the slave trade had recently been made illegal. Better late than never.

Other locals had owned slaves. In 1697, the death had occurred in Barbados of a Stratford man, Colonel Francis Russell. He died without leaving a will so his '50 Negroes' were treated as part of his real estate (property) and were therefore to go to his heir. Slaves frequently ended up as the 'property' of single women and widows who were thereby provided with an income from their slaves' efforts. When slavery was abolished many in this group faced poverty when compensation was not awarded

However Ann Trinder, a local woman, certainly benefited from slavery and it came about with the death of her relative Mr Thomas Trinder. He was a bachelor and an employee of the 'Company of Merchants Trading in Africa' set up in 1750 to 'facilitate Britain's Africa Trade'. He was an officer with the company and as such operated one of the nine notorious trading 'factories' or forts along the coast. These held the captured slaves pending the arrival of traders' ships bound for the sugar plantations in the West Indies. In 1775, when he was about to die he dictated his will with the treatment of his slaves very much in his mind - but it makes for uncomfortable reading.[22]

- He wanted Abimabat, 'a slave woman of and from Shantee be made free as though she has never been my property'. His executors were to pay her 'four small girl slaves as a legacy as well as four ounces of goods, two dukers of rum, a baft' (cotton fabric often used to buy slaves) and 'any gold of mine she may have with her'. This was in 'consideration of her fidelity and constant attendance on me'.

- He asked that a slave woman called Bumushu who he 'had by me' along with her 'two female children be made over to the company, to be considered as their property'. His view was 'this is not so much to continue them as slaves as to prevent them from being pillaged and plundered by the free natives which would be the case if they have no master'.

- To Deborah, a free woman, he left 'all the gold and diggiie beads she has of mine'. The beads were the glass beads used by the Europeans as money to buy goods and slaves. He also left her his specified male house slaves, three girl slaves and his pawns. Pawns were slaves given to him by a debtor and remained his property until the debt was cleared. She was to also receive a 'barrel of gunpowder, thirty gallons of rum and a piece of blue baft'. Her son was to get two small boy slaves.
- He rewarded his servant with 'a boy of four feet two inches'.
- His effects were to be realised and the interest from the capital given annually to his two nearest relations living somewhere in England.

There was considerable delay in tracing the two relatives and by the time they were tracked down one of them had died. Ann Trinder was found in 1779 and no doubt benefited from the small income from the capital. It would be interesting to know what happened to Deborah, Abimabat and Bumushu.

The Society for the Abolition of Slavery

Slavery had been loudly denounced in London during the 1770's but it was not until 1787 and the formation of the Society for the Abolition of Slavery that effective opposition had got under way. Pivotal to its success was the backing of the well organised Quaker movement. The name that we associate with reform is Mr William Wilberforce, but equally committed to the cause was Mr Thomas Clarkson whose stirring essay on slavery was published and freely distributed by the Society. He was said to have been 'the heart and soul of the campaign' and is believed to have travelled over 35,000 miles around the country on horseback, stirring up support.

He displayed leg irons, branding irons, shackles and all manner of barbaric tools used in the slave trade and held up posters showing how the slaves were packed into the ships on the 'middle passage', where one in eight died. On seeing these things people saw that, contrary to the myths spread by the pro-slavery lobby, the slaves were not grateful to be rid of their unhappy lives in Africa. Jane Austin at first disagreed with Clarkson's ideas but on reading one of his books 'fell in love with the author'.

Since a majority of men, and most women were without a vote, petitions became an attractive way of expressing their opinions. In 1787, the success of the first petition instigated by the Manchester Abolitionist Committee was encouraging. The Committee subsequently circulated an appeal to provincial newspapers and chief magistrates to raise their own petitions and it seems that one such was circulated by Stratford's Mayor, Mr William Eaves, in 1788 and signed by aldermen and burgesses. [23] It was addressed 'To the Commons of Great Britain in Parliament Assembled' and began by stating, 'That your petitioners being convinced that the traffic in the human species practiced by this Nation upon the Inhabitants of Africa cannot be justified upon any grounds' and continued, 'the rights of mankind are far superior to all considerations of private interest and commercial advantage'. They did 'pray that this deplorable traffic may no longer have continuance' and that it 'be entirely abolished'. It is uncertain that this petition was actually despatched. Similar petitions were more successfully supported elsewhere and two hundred in all were sent to Westminster, although not all were supportive of complete abolition.

Stratford tried again in March of 1792 when another Mayor, Mr Charles Ingram, had the Corporation Seal affixed to a nationally organised petition.[24] The petition was inspired by yet another failed anti-slavery Bill and was one of 519 petitions sent to Westminster on that occasion. In total just under 400,000 concerned people had signed.

Following the failure of the 1791 Abolition of Slavery Act, people not only signed more petitions but also began boycotting West Indies sugar. Sugar was the largest import by value compared with coffee, cotton and tobacco, where slave labour was also involved, so this made sense. Boycotting slave-plantation sugar became the thing to do and women took the lead, resulting in a drop in sales by as much as one third in some parts of England. The boycott must have been a hot topic of conversation in Stratford's fashionable coffee house on Wood Street where copious amounts of sugar were needed. Josiah Wedgwood's brooch depicting a slave woman saying 'Am I not a woman and a sister' was a popular way of advertising your opinion.

As early as 1729 the selling and buying of slaves in London and Liverpool to be used as servants was strongly criticised but not sufficiently to diminish the popular fashion for black servants. The whole issue of slavery within the United Kingdom was muddied by the lack of legislation *against* it. In 1772, following a much publicised court case, Lord Mansfield decreed that the slave, James Somersett, could not be forcibly removed from London and returned to his plantation. A group of freed slaves, called 'the sons of Africa', spoke publicly of their experiences in the sugar plantations. Olaudah Equiano, the most famous of them, wrote a book that became an instant best seller. With the true facts exposed, public opinion was beginning to shift. Stratford was far from immune to the common enthusiasm for reform. In 1790, a local widow, Mrs Jane Gastrell, bequeathed £100 to the Society for the Abolition of Slavery in her will. She was not alone in doing this. Finally in 1807 with the passing of the Slave Trade Act the trade in slaves throughout the British Empire was finally abolished.

The arrest in Stratford of Mr William Smith, in 1821, said a lot about the value attached to sugar. He was tried at the Petty Sessions for attempting to trick a Stratford woman, Mrs Mary Kendall, with a bag of dirt. She thought that her fifty-six shillings were buying one hundredweight of sugar in a sack; she was in fact buying a sack of soil topped by eight ounces of sugar. This caused a 'great damage and deception of the said Joseph Kendall', Mary's husband, who attended court because the money exchanged was his - under the then law his wife could not own money. [25] Smith's act of deception was only possible because the country had developed an incredibly sweet tooth in the preceding century. In 1830 the flourishing river trade, which came up the Avon from Bristol via the Gloucester Docks and the Gloucester and Sharpness Canal was said to be 'principally from the

West Indies'. It is hoped that Mr Smith's eight ounces of sugar did not involve slave labour - but it probably did.

The Slave Trade Compensation Commission

If the trade in slaves was made illegal by the 1807 Slave Trade Act the battle to end slavery continued for a further twenty-six years, until the passing of the 1833 Slavery Abolition Act. After several more years of divided opinion the controversial, but pragmatic, Slave Trade Compensation Commission was established. This was to facilitate compensation payments to slave owners within the British Empire, for their loss of income. Ten civil servants spent four years compiling ledgers that contained the names of the 46,000 slave owners. By 1837 when the paperwork was completed, the Commission offered £15 million and finally agreed to £20 million, which in today's money would be £17 billion. It was the biggest bail-out in British history until the 2009 bank pay-out. With 50% of the total payments paid to 6% of the claimants it made a few wealthy people even wealthier. The £4 million invested in the burgeoning railway system at this time, so fuelling 'railway mania', came from these payments and arguably the whole country benefited. In Warwickshire there were thirty-one separate claims.[26] Mr Robert Sympson, of Leamington Spa, possibly a lawyer acting for a collective, made the most claims - for 1,703 slaves - in Jamaica. They earned compensation in excess of £35,316. Mrs Eleanor Tringham, also of Leamington, unsuccessfully claimed £6,526 2s 0d for the loss of 256 slaves in Grenada. (Her claim may have failed because her husband, William, was claiming for the same slaves).

Unfortunately, the 1833 Act did not abolish slavery in America where slave labour was extensively used in the cotton fields. In a letter, dated 1838 from South Carolina, the author, Mr Thomas Cooper, wrote 'we cannot work the rich Southern soil with white free labour' and 'If you want cotton manufacture then you have to have them'. He was writing to Sir George Philips, a very wealthy Lancashire cotton-mill owner who lived in nearby Long Compton and whose relatives erected the obelisk on Stratford's Welcombe Fields. Philips's great wealth had been gained through the connection between imported raw cotton (involving slave labour) and cheap labour in his factories (involving women and children). He was no lover of factory reform, accusing those who were of 'cant and hypocrisy'.[27] He was now being told politely that he had a vested interest in the continued use of slaves.

It would seem odd that Philips was protesting at the use of slave labour for since 1817 he had received an income from a sugar plantation in Jamaica and had made an unsuccessful compensation claim for £1,904 19s 10d for the 108 slaves involved. He may well have been dismayed to discover that the use of slave labour in the cotton fields had increased and was expressing his concern. The more pragmatic Cooper reminded him that 'all slave states are the friends of Great Britain and eminently her customers and consumers'. Cooper added that his slaves 'are upon the whole the happiest slaves'. With this level of understanding of the slaves' lot, the cotton trade was able to continue using slave labour in the United States long after the passing of both the 1807 and 1833 Acts.

Chapter 7

The Morris Family

The land awarded to John Keen in 1775 provided sufficient income for him to live a comfortable life. But the Morris family required something different. By 1801 three sons, Samuel, Joel and John, had reached the age of twenty-one and their parents wanted to hand over a large amount of money to each one in order to 'promote their advancement in the world'. The relatively low income from the inherited land did not allow this and John Keen's complicated will stood in the way - as he had intended.

The industrial revolution was well under way and nearby industrial Birmingham offered the opportunity to acquire great wealth so it was there that Mary and Joel's thoughts turned for their three sons. Unfortunately, the terms of John Keen's will meant that the property had to descend to the grandchildren intact. In 1800 Samuel, Joel, John and their parents took decisive action: they borrowed the huge sum of £1,000 from a widow, Constance Wroughton of Edgbaston, using the inherited land and house as a form of security. The money was then shared between the three sons. Obviously they could not repay the £1,000 in the stipulated year, along with the 5% interest, and they were bound to be taken to court, and that was exactly what happened.

In 1801 the family was issued with a recovery summons from the Court of Chancery in London 'so that full seizure of tenements and common' could take place.[28] The summons was an impressive document with an equally impressive red wax seal attached via a long red ribbon, so large that, for its protection, it was placed in a round tin box with a lid. The Chancery Court heard cases of inheritance that were problematic and the Morris' case certainly fitted the bill but the Court was notorious for its slow pace, its backlog of cases and for its extortionate costs. Dickens, in *Bleak House*, damns it for its incompetence and corruption - and that was at a later time when it had been reformed. When the Morris' case was due to appear it was grinding almost to a standstill. The whole business was further complicated when, in 1802, son John, one of the beneficiaries died.

In 1803 an assignment document was issued by the Morris family when they 'did bargain, sell, assign, and release and for ever quit claim and confirm unto Charles Glover all the abstracted premises and appurtenances'. But it was not until January 1808 when the property was finally 'released to Mr John Alexander' that the affair could be settled. Then all five remaining grandchildren (both parents being dead) 'do bargain sell release and confirm unto John Alexander' all the lands of John Keen so that he 'became perfect tenant of freehold' so that 'a good and perfect common recovery or recoveries might be thereof had'. They did so at a cost of five shillings each. His payment of one peppercorn made him 'in actual possession of all'. A 'common recovery' could be used collaboratively in this way to 'bar' a 'fee entail' that Keen's will had imposed. Tenants, such as Mr Alexander had become, could sell land and that is exactly what he did, and he did it swiftly. Some land and property was immediately sold off whilst the remainder went to auction in 1809 (*see* Chapter 9).

The family had been receiving rental income from their grandfather's Henley Street house by leasing it out. In October they sold it to one George Barke, for £350. He pulled it down in 1810 and rebuilt it, adding two stables. The Morris's probably did not much care what happened to their grand-father's house; they had at last acquired a sizable sum of money from his property and could be certain that more, a lot more, was about to follow.

To recap: in 1801, when the Morris's wanted £1,000 they had purposefully placed their inheritance in jeopardy by using it as security for a loan. They were, as a result of defaulting on their repayments, burdened by a debt that was growing at the rate of 5% per annum and had been obliged to appear in a court that had the power to settle such complicated muddles. They employed, at no doubt great expense, a London lawyer to plead their case and could not have known that the process would take over six years. Now, in 1808, with Mr Alexander in charge, their inheritance went to auction but with no guarantee that their total indebtedness would be covered.

John Keen's dream that his estate would grow in size and prestige as it passed down succeeding generations had been destroyed, initially by the death of his only son then later by the actions of his son-in-law and grandchildren, ably assisted by the legal profession.

Chapter 8

The Post

When the Morris family waited impatiently for news from their lawyer in London they were dependent on a rackety postal system. In Stratford, the efficient delivery of letters, after reform of the postal system in 1840, helped local businesses to thrive. However with the emergence of the Bard-related tourist business in the 1850's it became a matter of much wider public concern. Many concluded that the main post office was an embarrassing eyesore which harmed the town's reputation. The solution was to cause anguish to the resident postmaster Mr John Reupert Guppy, more of him later.

Charles I had opened the Royal Mail service for public use in 1635 and it had remained almost unaltered over the years with single riders, called 'post-boys', delivering letters to postmasters who forwarded them to the recipient who was then required to pay for the service. Post boys were notoriously slow, averaging just three miles per hour, and were very vulnerable to attack. Often, they were drunk and there were many stories of mail bags being cut from post horses whilst they were tethered outside inns. Stratford was a centre for the post: the post-boys arrived and the postmaster or mistress retrieved the local mail before sending them on to Henley, Alcester and Redditch. The process was slow, corrupt and unreliable, and it was costly with recipients frequently returning letters unopened if they didn't like the look of them, or they did not like the sender or they simply could not afford to pay.

The increased number of turnpike roads during the eighteenth century allowed for the later introduction of Royal Mail Coaches. Journeys that had previously taken the post-boys two days to complete could be done in seventeen hours - and with increased speed the likelihood of hold-ups by highwaymen markedly declined. Delay was no longer tolerated and the mailbags were routinely flung in and out of moving coaches so as to save time. Passengers travelling in or on these early 'stage' coaches had a far from pleasant experience with boards at the windows and no springs. When springs were introduced they were a mixed blessing because they caused much sickness. Despite these drawbacks, passengers crammed into the coaches with many more clinging dangerously to the outside. In 1783 a Bill proposed limiting the numbers allowed to travel in this alarming way; it failed.

But with improved design and with the Royal Mail acquiring its own fleet of coaches at the beginning of the nineteenth century, things improved. The mail carriages were by then impressive vehicles with black and maroon livery, the Royal Crest on both doors and wheels painted scarlet (the colour lives on today). Sitting on top of these fine coaches would be a driver and guard, dressed in scarlet coats with blue lapels edged with gold braid. The guard had two pistols and a blunderbuss to hand and, rather oddly, was the only Royal Mail employee. He had to remain with the mail box for the complete journey and, as a result, in the winter months guards sometimes froze to death, or so it was said.

Horses and driver were changed every ten to fifteen miles and, initially, the provision of horses and a driver was contracted out, a potentially lucrative business for the contractor. Mr Burke, a local man, invested heavily in it hoping to make his fortune but he misunderstood the complexity of the finances involved and in 1817 he went bankrupt. Providing the service may well have made one or two people rich but most of those involved in the business - ostlers, coachmen and guards - were poorly paid. Tipping was expected and complaining was best avoided. Guarding the Royal Mail however was always taken seriously and in 1854 a local, Mr William Hartiss, appeared in court for allowing someone to 'ride in the place appointed for the guard'. He was fined £20. Fortunately, this draconian sum was 'remitted' later by a more kindly JP.

Stratford's postmasters and postmistresses

As the Royal Mail coach arrived at Clopton Bridge the guard blasted away on the horn to ensure that the toll gate was opened in advance.

Postmasters were frequently the local inn keepers as they could stable and change horses efficiently as well as provide a safe space for the mail. Mr Payton of the White Lion Inn fitted the bill when he became the post master in 1779 hence its long connection with Stratford's early post office. Individuals often came to collect their letters, rather than waiting for a post-boy to deliver to their door. Gradually, the depositing of mail in such places as inns came to be seen as bad practice and separate post offices were required, as happened in Stratford.

The identity of the postmasters went unrecorded following the death of Mr Payton in 1780 but it was probable that tenant innkeepers assumed the role until Mrs Smith arrived. Detail of her career is limited to her retirement in 1808 when she was succeeded by Mr John Lane who continued to find accommodation in the White Lion until he relocated next door to a building at the western tip of Henley Street (Fig 2 No. 32). Mr Lane must have anticipated a secure future because he bought the building for £430.

From then on, he, and subsequently Mrs Joanna Meredith and Mr John Guppy, followed the rather odd custom of providing their own premises as the Post Office. They were paid a rent allowance by the government until 1892 when the practice came to an acrimonious end.

Before he could take office Mr Lane was required to swear an oath before the Mayor, John Tasker, a local JP. He promised not to 'delay or detain' any of the post that came into his hands nor to 'embezzle any such Letter or Letters, Packet or Packets'.[29] The swearing of such oaths was part of an effort to stop widespread pilfering and it increased public confidence in George III's Royal Mail.

Whilst running the post office Mr Lane was inevitably involved in employing the notoriously slow post-boys. Their role had changed as the mail coaches took over but they were still needed to deliver letters to nearby villages. One of Stratford's post-boys, John Bury, was called to appear as a witness at a Quarter Session held in 1829.[30] James Pritchard, a 'chaise driver', pleaded guilty to stealing a 'Drab greatcoat' valued at £2 10s 0d from a post-boy, William Read, over in Warwick. He had taken the coat from the stables in the Warwick Arms and fled speedily to the Swan and Maidenhead Inn, Stratford, where he offered it to John Bury. The Swan and Maidenhead Inn was situated close to the White Lion on Henley Street where John was employed. James persuaded John that it was a suitable coat for a post-boy and told him that he had bought it in London but was now hard up. They agreed a price of sixteen shillings and a quart of ale. All went well for James until John put the coat on and felt in the pockets. He pulled out a letter and 'a character' (a reference). James said it was there because he was hoping to apply to become the 'Boot' at the George inn at Shipston but John recognised the letter as belonging to William Read, whom he knew to be a post-boy in Warwick. He promptly called Constable William Joy and James was arrested. Although James pleaded guilty he certainly would have faced jail. These were hard times and sentencing reform was still a long way off.

Postal reform

The system continued unaltered until the arrival, in 1840, of Rowland Hill's Penny Black stamps. Mr Lane and his wife had run the post office for thirty-two years when the great change occurred. They were both sixty-four years old, had been married for forty years, brought up five children and perhaps were wanting a quieter life. But this was not to be - quite the reverse. Mr Lane was required to sell the new one-penny stamps and he had never been busier. Before Hill's changes, the recipient of a letter was charged according to the number of sheets used and the distance travelled. With the letter folded and sealed with wax there was no need of an envelope and they did not appear for another five or so years. The cost of a letter could be as much as one shilling (approx. £5 today) and letters were frequently returned unopened. Now responsibility for payment was reversed and, with an initial print run of 68,808,000 Penny Black stamps, all was set for the big change. The postal system became both efficient and profitable almost overnight and the population fell in love with letter writing in their thousands, if not millions, using Penny Blacks in vast numbers.

The young queen Victoria featured on the stamps and Rowland Hill was knighted for bringing them into being.

Hopefully all this increased activity did not cause the death of Mrs Lane who died just two years later. But Mr Lane lived on and had to deal with the ever-increasing flow of letters. Prior to the change his quarterly return sheets had shown that the loss made on 'returned letters' reached a peak of £31 10s 2d in 1838. In January 1840, three months prior to the introduction of the stamps, he was given a pay rise and by the end of May he must have realised why; he now had to cut round hundreds of adhesive black stamps, charge the one penny and post-mark them. By the next quarter his salary figure was upped yet again, to £33 5s 0d, reflecting the change in his employment. The humble 'letter carriers' also experienced an increased work-load but their grievances were not addressed until July 1841 when their total cost increased, indicating either a pay rise or simply that more of them were employed. Meanwhile the cost of 'returned letters' fell to just £2 15s 9d by July 1840. A short while later Mr Lane, on his own initiative, set about checking the volume of letters passing through his office. It was probably as a result of this scrutiny that he was given yet another pay rise.

Mr Lane continued working until he died in 1854, aged seventy-eight. The following year on the 24th July, the post-office building, his home, went to auction at the White Lion. All trace of it vanished when it was pulled down by the Corporation in1928 to widen the road.

In 1856, shortly after the death of Mr Lane, Mrs Joanna Meredith was sworn in as the postmistress. She was a young widow with three children from Henley in Arden. She chose to run her business from 52 Henley Street (Fig 2 No. 19) and, for the first time, the post office was no longer in close association with an inn. Why she resigned is unknown but by 1871 Mr Guppy had taken her place. Three years previously cats had been appointed by the government as official rat and mouse catchers for the Royal Mail. An allowance of one shilling a week per cat was given to the felines in London and, amidst much wrangling, a lower allowance for their provincial relatives. It can only be hoped that Mrs Meredith did not leave the service on account of the employment of a cat.

Mr John Reupert Guppy

The new postmaster and his family were soon established in the rented property vacated by Mrs Meredith. The building was situated on the eastern corner of Henley Street with Meer Street, since demolished when Meer Street was widened. Mr John Reupert Guppy and his wife Jane had arrived from Exeter twenty years earlier as newly-weds when he had been employed as the schoolmaster in the National School for Boys on the Alcester Road. They had four daughters Helen, Georgina, Catherine and Emily. Over the years running the post office became a family business with the Guppy daughters brought in as assistants when their formal education was completed.

Postmasters gained status when they were entrusted with responsibility for the registration of births and deaths but this did not protect Mr Guppy's tenure from repeated troubles. It began in 1872 when his 'letter carriers' were criticised for being 'indistinguishable from ordinary day labourers or petty chapmen' and it was suggested that their appearance could be improved by 'providing them with a livery authorised by the post master general'.[31] But this was minor compared to the level of criticism of the state of the post-office building. It was an issue that would bedevil Mr Guppy, particularly towards the end of his life when he was not in the best of health.

As early as 1882, more 'suitable and efficient accommodation' was thought to be necessary and the idea that the Corporation should intervene was mooted for the first time. It must be remembered that the post office was also Mr Guppy's home and unfortunately it was situated in a rough part of Henley Street, close to slum housing. The issue of its suitability rumbled on until 1888. It was then thought inappropriate that the premises of a Government office should be privately owned and the Government was duly brought into the debate. Nothing happened and everyone was 'at sixes and sevens' over the business.[32] Various buildings were suggested and opinion became heated. A petition was circulated.

Fig 14. The grand new post office, 42 Sheep Street 1892

The local press, the *Herald,* opined that 'there is no town in the whole of the kingdom… that has a shabbier and more inconvenient post office'.[33] At last, in 1890 a new state-of-the-art post office was commissioned for £2,228. To everyone's relief it finally opened in 1892 (Fig 14 & Fig 2 No. 10) and the lofty Elizabethan styled building at 42 Sheep Street became an 'ornament to the town'.[34] The conveyance document was signed by the Post Master General in London - the days when postmasters opened their homes to the public were finally over.

The change in ownership of post offices came too late for the gentle Mr Guppy who wrote his will in March 1889 and after a painful illness was dead a year later. The town mourned him and his coffin was escorted to the church by all the letter carriers of the town and district, probably wearing their smart blue livery. Mr Guppy's widow and her one remaining unmarried daughter Emily were required to immediately leave their rented post-office accommodation. Mrs Jane

Guppy died in 1892 perhaps worn down by the changes. The home that she was required to leave so unceremoniously was temporarily occupied by her husband's successor while the new post office building was completed. And there was an additional humiliation: her husband's replacement was Mrs Elizabeth Bordeaux, a fifty-six-year-old widow who had several of her thirteen children living with her. This must also have seemed particularly harsh to twenty-nine-year old Emily who had spent her adult life running the post office with her father and was perfectly capable of continuing to run it.

Both women would have been aware that a government ruling stated that only experienced *men* could hold such senior positions. If Mrs Bordeaux's appointment shocked Mrs Guppy and Emily it also shocked a lot of people in town. A letter published in the *Herald*, written by a furious post-office clerk, explains why.[35] He and his poorly paid colleagues sought advancement through the official circular, it being the usual course 'adopted in filling vacancies'. The understanding was that only 'a man who has grown up in the service' would be considered for such promotion. But a widow 'who has no claim to the position and no ability… who knows little or nothing of the business' had been handed the job. As such he was of the opinion that she would offer 'poor service to the residents of Stratford'. He signed, 'One who has grown grey in service'. He urged the Mayor and corporation to ask the Post Master General for an explanation.

Mrs Bordeaux managed to remain in post for five years before passing the responsibility on to her eldest daughter, Elizabeth. However, Elizabeth was obliged to retire in 1901, at the age of forty, when she became Mrs William Doonan. This was in accordance with the 'marriage bar' which excluded married women from professional employment. Mr Doonan was one of her sorting clerks and via marriage (note, not via the official circular!) he had become the post master. Despite ill health, Mr Doonan was postmaster until around 1913.

With the First World War came reports of national concern about the probable demise of the national postal service caused by the conscription of key workers. The solution was the removal of restrictions on the employment of women. Within the first two years of the war 35,000 women were recruited, thereby saving the nation's postal system. Once the war was over they were promptly 'released' from their employment.

Miss Emily Guppy must have watched this unfold with very mixed emotions. On leaving her home and her busy life in the post office she spent the next fifty years as a boarder at various addresses in Leamington Spa 'living off private means' thanks to her father's investments. For a single woman, such as Emily this would have meant leading an increasingly frugal life to ensure that the 'private means' did not run out prematurely.

Chapter 9

The 1809 Auction

On the 26th and 27th September 1809 at 3pm, in the White Lion Inn, an auction was held to sell the portion of John Keen's land that is the subject of this story, the land to the east of Guild Pitts and close to the Warwick Road. Posters (Fig 15) displayed a plan showing the twenty-seven plots, 'intended roads' and a description of the land. John Keen had died nineteen years earlier, his grandchildren were now more than willing to settle the whole business. They were:

- Samuel Morris a hosier, married to Theodoria living in Stockport.
- Joel Morris junior a chandler, married to Mary (and then Nancy) living in West Bromwich.
- Elizabeth, married to Benjamin Reddell a sword-cutler living in Birmingham.
- Mary, married to John Nock a traveller living in West Bromwich.
- Thomas Morris a button maker, married to Ann, sister to John Nock, living in Birmingham.

Fig 15. The plan for the 1809 auction

In 1808 the five grandchildren had finally won control over their inheritance. As noted, the delay had been caused by John Keen's restrictive and complicated will which had caused the family to turn to the notorious Court of Chancery, possibly at great cost. Because the £1,000 loan, taken on in 1801, had not been paid off they were gambling that the auction would raise enough money to clear the debt *and* make them rich.

Auctioning as a means of selling property and goods was a relatively new practice. The famous auction houses of Sotheby's and Christies in London were well established but in Stratford there was no such venue. Local inns served the purpose and in Stratford the White Lion Inn was a favoured location. John Keen's land had been divided into 'Lots' that would appear attractive to different interested parties. There were the very large plots that would be expected to remain in their 'high state of cultivation'; these would appeal to those who were happy to lease the land out to small-holders. There was also the attraction of the 'excellent Mine of Clay under the Whole of it' that would allow speculation for any business-minded person who might consider a profitable brick works as an investment. Then there were the very small plots along the 'intended road', soon to be called Great William Street. These would have appealed to builders and developers who would eventually turn that side of town into New Town Ward, *the* place to live. At this point the Mayfield Avenue land can be seen defined as Lot 13 (adjoining Lots 11 and 14 associated with later development).

The family were not as dependent on this auction as would first appear. In September 1808, very soon after the courts granted Mr John Alexander the authority to sell the inheritance, they had several windfalls. John Keen's river-side land was sold to Thomas Tasker for £730. Additionally, the Henley Street house was sold to the unsentimental George Barke for £350 (*see* Chapter 3). The grandchildren had also made an agreement with George Lloyd for the sale of 'four closes' containing forty-three acres, two roods and three perches for £3,000.[36] This huge acreage was the land situated towards Bishopton, awarded to John Keen during inclosure. It was not going to be part of the auction but implicit in the transaction was that £1,000 be paid immediately to Mr Charles Glover 'out of the respective shares of the five grandchildren'. This was to pay off the outstanding loan that Glover had been responsible for since 1803. By the 27th September 1808 it had all been paid over to him, and the family were free of the debt. The remaining £2,000 was to be equally divided between the remaining five grandchildren. They had, it would seem, managed to pay off the annual interest as it accrued over the years. As a result of these three sales the grandchildren had already received a total of £4,080 and with the original debt repaid they must have felt a huge sense of relief.

On the day of the auction in September 1809, Mr John Fetherston, a victualler, bought Lots 11 and 13 along with other lots for £736.[37] Present day Mayfield Avenue extends up through the middle of Lot 13, which was then 'highly cultivated land'. Having successfully bid at the auction in September, he acquired it on the 29th December via a lease agreement and completed the deal the next day, as was the custom - on the 30th December. Lot 14, the remainder of Mayfield Avenue land, was sold on the same day to Mr John Manton, a plumber and glazier, for £270 'of lawful English money'.[38] He too purchased and completed on the same two days in December having borrowed the money from Mr William Stephens, a farmer. To secure the sale, the interested parties would enter into a lease agreement, often involving a peppercorn.

These three Lots raised a total of £750. When added to the already pocketed £4,080, the resulting £5,086 surely settled the question as to whether the Morris children would be able to pay off their debt and live comfortably. But their lawyer's and court costs could have jeopardised things somewhat. With the Court of Chancery's reputation for exorbitant fees it can only be hoped that they were able to pay up and be happy with the final outcome.

With the exception of Lots 26 and 27, the new owners of Mr Keen's land can be identified.

- Mr Thomas Sharshaw and Mr Thomas Tasker, both butchers bought Lots 1, 2, 5 and 6 for £470.
- Mr Samuel Field, a baker bid successfully for Lots 3, 4, 7, 8 and 9 for £1,270.

- Mr Enoch Buttwell, a draper bought Lot 10 for £265.
- Mr Thomas Court bought Lots 22, 23 and 24 for £99.
- Mr John Fetherston, the victualler, also bought Lots 17-21 for £480.
- Mr William Burman, grocer bought Lot 25 and probably also Lots 26 and 27.
- Mr Samuel Manison, a druggist (or possibly a grocer) bought Lots 15 and 16 comprising 3,000 square feet 'more or less' for £115. He certainly made a handsome profit, when in 1813 he sold just a part of Lot 16 for £110. This speculative buying was replicated elsewhere.

Adding all known sales, the total figure came to £7,785, with the final figure being in excess of this. It is difficult to estimate the wealth of the siblings in modern terms but a conservative guess might put it at well over £800,500. Suffice it to say that they ended up very rich. They finally had a substantial amount of cash in their pockets and the land John Keen had tried so hard to protect was now divided between a draper, a butcher, a druggist, a plumber, a grocer and very many others.

With this auction the five remaining grandchildren had finally received their inheritance. They were:

Samuel Morris was listed in 1808 as a 'gentleman' and so was probably already a wealthy man. His earlier share of the £1,000 loan, taken out by his parents, had certainly 'advanced' his prospects because he moved to Stockport, Manchester, where he plied a very successful business as a hosier. The proceeds of the auction would have only added to his wealth.

Joel Morris settled in West Bromwich and in 1818 was described as a 'tallow chandler' - which entailed making candles from sheep fat. Since 'town gas' for lighting was not generally available until around 1836, his income was secure. It is probably safe to assume he was an employer given the money he had received from his parents.

Elizabeth Morris married Benjamin Reddell in 1802 and lived in Birmingham where Benjamin was listed as a 'sword cutler'. Later he became a 'bottle jack maker'. His business was in *the* centre of the metal industry and as Elizabeth had not benefitted from the £1,000 loan it is clear that he had achieved his success on his own initiative. However, the acquisition of several thousand pounds following the 1809 auction must have been welcome.

Mary Morris married John Nock from Birmingham. He was described as a 'traveller' by occupation. A contemporary definition in *Webster's Dictionary* states that a traveller was a 'travelling mercantile clerk' which meant travelling extensively in the very lively stage coaches. Hopefully the windfall that came their way in 1809 enabled them to lead an easier life.

Thomas Morris, the last child to be born into the family, was too young to have benefited from the £1,000 loan. He married a Birmingham woman, Ann Nock, in 1808 just months before the auction. The couple settled in West Bromwich where Thomas was a button maker. He probably did better than all his brothers because he was involved in a business in which fortunes were being made and Birmingham was at the heart of the trade. He was in the business before machinery was introduced, which threatened small businesses such as his, and was able to retire to leafy Dudley.

Chapter 10

Law and Order

The early nineteenth century was a time when many families left the land to find work in the new factories. They crowded into the towns and cities where crime and unruly behaviour steeply increased. The government became concerned for the future of the country and this concern was shared by the worthies of Stratford, a concern that was heightened whenever they thought control of their police force was to be curtailed. Responsibility for law enforcement had historically been down to local initiative and whenever changes were imposed, by the Government or the County, they were met with a lot of foot dragging and a great deal of anger.

Stratford had had its constables since medieval times and later had an organised system of night-watchmen overseen by a Watch Committee. Stratford Borough Police Records of 1760 and 1765 show that the borough was served by a rota of six constables. This system of watch patrols continued into the early 1800s and reflects the national reluctance to accept a professional police force. If there was serious trouble a local JP would 'read the riot act' (*see* Chapter 4) and the local militia would arrive to support the constables. The fact that this was an unpopular and heavy-handed remedy was largely ignored because it was effective when things got tough.

The 1818 enquiry
In 1814 the Secretary of State's Office, directed by Lord Sidmouth, sent a letter to towns and cities in Britain requesting information on the number of persons charged 'with felony and misdemeanour... if no persons come to trial I do desire you to nevertheless make a return'.[39] This was the first of a string of such enquiries that flowed from London, the start of an understanding by government that good governance depended on accurate information, and it was probably the replies that prompted a government enquiry four years later, in 1818. The enquiry looked into the levels of criminality revealed by the

61

new data and which could not now be ignored. There were various arguments put forward as to the cause but the establishment of a national police force was not yet an option; prevailing opinion held that 'we live in a free society' and that a national police force would mitigate against this.

If there was alarm in the capital and other large cities it was relatively calm in Stratford where constable Robert Cooper, was doing what was necessary in a way that had been unchanged for very many years. In March 1818 he took Richard Beach, the local wheelwright, to the Borough Court for riotous behaviour, although the behaviour was hardly riotous as it involved Beach refusing to pay for a pint of beer as he had 'no money to pay'.[40] He also refused to leave the pub and finally shook his fists at the constable, saying he would 'stop as long as he pleased'. Three weeks later, in early April, Cooper personally took action at the local Quarter Sessions against Beach for assault 'on his person' whilst on duty. Respect for the constabulary was essential to the rule of law and the court would ensure that he had it when arresting villains. Later in November Cooper must have felt less happy at having to attend the Borough Court, being charged with negligently allowing a prisoner, Robert Ainge, to escape.

Whether this event undermined confidence in his authority is not clear but, by 1820, residents were reassessing the quality of their protection. A letter expressed concern about 'The many degridations that have lately been committed in the town' and therefore the need to establish a more effective nightly watch.[41] It was suggested that residents could take turns going on watch and 'those that can't to pay for each night that is their turn'. Those with the money preferred to pay. A year later contributions from the wealthier residents totalled £22 1s 6d and Mr Matthew Mole had become the police constable and was paid a salary from these subscriptions. It would appear that the idea of a rota of residents acting as part-time law-enforcers lacked appeal. In his first year he successfully prosecuted Mr William Mallins, an unfortunate poacher caught 'possessed of a hare for selling' whilst using a greyhound. [42] Having a greyhound was illegal 'unless of clearly defined personage'. Rather suspiciously just eight days later he prosecuted Mr William Pritchard for keeping 'one dog called a grey hound to kill and destroy game'. Both men were fined £5. Hopefully these arrests satisfied those who were now paying his wages.

However around this time, given the steep increase in the town's population and in the incidence of crime (*see* Chapter 4), it was reluctantly agreed that there was a problem. The solution was to recruit three full-time paid constables, under the authority of JPs, who could respond more reliably and promptly to incidents of law breaking, and so in 1824, Constables Hobbins, Heritage and Ashfield joined Constable Cooper. The newly appointed Constable John Ashfield's routine cases concerned horse stealing, driving carts without reins, begging, theft, breach of the peace, receiving stolen peas and beans and several cases of non-payment of rates and non-payment of child maintenance. If there was increasing lawlessness and gang culture elsewhere in the cities of nineteenth-century England, in Stratford crime was pretty tame stuff.

The crimes that the local constables were handling may have been trivial but the punishments weren't. Mr Beechey, a local man, following an appearance at the Quarter Sessions, was transported to Australia for fourteen years for stealing '5 fowls'. In 1828 *The Warwickshire General Advertiser* reported that John Williams, was sentenced at the Warwick Assize to transportation for life for stealing a piece of mutton. John Highfield was hanged for forgery and another man for illegally returning from transportation. Children were not exempt. In 1825, the *Herald*, reported the flogging of two boys 'Samuel Edwards and his friend Wheeler' for stealing pears from Mr Hawkes and Mr Buckingham.

Sir Robert Peel

In the summer of 1828 all the constables in England were required by the Government to count every 'lunatic pauper' on their watch. Constable George Hobbins, the day-constable in Stratford, set about the task.[42] This was one of a string of such requests that flowed from

London throughout the 1830s. Others requested the numbers of bastard children, homicides and deaths by poison. When the results were in, the government deduced that the much-feared 'under class' *was* evolving in the cities. The 'lower orders' should be a peaceable lot reliably fit and able to turn up for work in the factories; something had to be done.

As early as 1829 Sir Robert Peel, as Home Secretary, against strong opposition, provided the solution for London. He created the first unified salaried police force, the Metropolitan Police. Until then there had been an assortment of independently funded law enforcers such as the Bow Street Runners. The crime rate fell and the 'Bobbies' or 'Peelers' became a welcome sight. Peel had set the template for a change that would eventually be repeated elsewhere in the country. His idea was that the force should be primarily preventative and a superintendent's success should be measured not by the number of arrests his constables made, but by the lack of crime in his area. Peel was especially keen that his men should mingle with population, and their distinctive top hats (strong enough to stand on) and frock coats with high collars (to prevent strangulation) certainly ensured this. He did not want the uniform to have military associations but the choice of blue unfortunately led to his men being called 'raw lobsters' (military uniform at the time was predominately red and soldiers were called 'lobsters').

The 1839 County Police Act created a new set of 'Rules and Regulations' aimed at 'establishing an uniform system for the government, pay, clothing accoutrements and necessaries of constables' not just in London but across the country. By 1840 'recommendations' regarding a national uniform arrived in Stratford.[43] Each constable was to have a cape and a great-coat, both with a badge, two pairs of trousers, a pair of boots and shoes, a hat and a stock, a belt and a pair of gloves. For protection there was a staff and a pair of handcuffs. If in real danger, a policeman could use a cutlass.

The recently formed Watch Committee had already decided on their own uniform back in 1836. It consisted of a blue coat with a plain collar, Oxford grey trousers, black oilskin cape, an oilskin hat and a pair of stout boots. Later modifications brought the Stratford police more into line with the national requirements. The constables were probably a welcome sight as they strolled in and out of the police station on Sheep Street (Fig 2 No. 8). In 1879 Mr Robert Guy in Bridge Street provided the over-coats for the three constables at £1 13s 0d each. Mr Sharman, on Union Street, supplied the hats at 10s and Mr Rider, on High Street, the night-belts at 3s 0d and dress-belts at 10s each. The photo of Thomas Rowley (Fig 16) then aged fifty-six, c.1880, shows the uniform - worn with some aplomb and with facial hair that perhaps enhanced his authority.

Fig 16. Portrait of Chief of Police Thomas Rowley c.1880

The Borough Police

In January 1836 Stratford's Borough Police Force came into being following the 1835 Municipal Corporations Act. The newly formed Watch Committee was responsible for appointing the new constables and they did so at their first meeting. The force consisted of Superintendent Thomas Taylor and five constables. The two day constables were George Mann and Joseph Reason, both paid 7s per week. The three night constables, paid 10s per week, were Samuel Allbone, John Watts and James Byerley. Superintendent Thomas Taylor's pay was set at £1 per week. His day began at 9pm and ended at 6am. He was responsible for organising the 'beats', checking that they were being conducted well, delivering clear instructions, keeping account of the bail monies and 'generally using his discretion'. He had to be not less than five feet seven inches tall 'without his shoes' and 'not exceed 40 years'. He was to 'devote his whole time to the police service' and by 1855 being 'generally intelligent' and 'free from bodily complaint and of a strong constitution' was added to his job description. Meanwhile the constables' behaviour was to be impeccable, both on and off duty. They were directed on 'no account go into any inn, public house or beer house unless in the execution of duty' and were never to get into debt. Whilst doing the 'beat' they had to be 'firm and cautious' but when taking action they had to do so 'fearlessly and with decision'. Promotion was to be 'through the ranks'. Bravery could be rewarded with extra money but only with a JP's approval.

The expanded force took a while to settle down. By April Constable George Mann had been sacked for neglecting his duty leaving Constable Reason as the only day constable. In July John Watts gave notice and his replacement, William Barnes lasted just seven months. Internal trouble flared in 1837 when a new constable, John Wright, accused Superintendent Taylor of negligence. He failed to substantiate his complaint and was sacked instead. The force gradually settled down but trouble resurfaced in 1841 when Reason was temporarily suspended for unreasonable behaviour and Allbone was cautioned for being drunk. Constable Reason was in trouble again in 1846 when he briefly left town and was required to forfeit his wages to the replacement constable, and again a year later when he requested extra pay. Troublesome though he was, Reason was never fired. Perhaps recruitment was difficult since the wages were set low and the job was arduous. When Allbone and Taylor left the force in 1857, it was recorded that both had 'become worn out by length of service'.[44]

Stratford gained the impressive County Petty Session House with a 'lock up' on the corner of Guild Street and Great William Street (Fig 2 No. 27). This was not an entirely trouble-free venture since the newly appointed Super-intending Constable Joseph Mayfield, recruited from Aston Manor, resigned just six months into the job.

The salary of £1 0s 0d per week, with two shillings extra for 'coals and candles' may not have satisfied. And so Joseph Reason, the long serving if slightly recalcitrant Stratford constable, was appointed in November 1849 being 'well qualified to take such a situation'.[45] With this promotion he moved from his home in Ely Street, one of the poorest streets in Stratford, into the grand County Petty Session House.

The 1855 Police Bill

Change came with the unpopular 1855 Police Bill, which was fiercely fought in Stratford and across the country because local authorities saw it as eroding their authority. A letter expressed local feeling: it was 'an unjustifiable attempt to interfere with local government' and an attempt to 'create a national police'.[46] But the Bill went through anyway. A poster in town asserted that the inhabitants of Stratford were 'particularly well satisfied with their own police force'. The subsequent amalgamation of the County Constabulary with the Stratford Borough Police, as a result of the 1855 Act, was greatly resented by Stratford's JPs.

Superintendent Joseph Reason lost his job a year later due to the changes. He was greatly respected because of his long and distinguished career which had begun back in 1829. The local JPs, led by the Mayor Dr David Price, organised a collection amongst themselves as he was left without a pension. He lived out the rest of his days as the innkeeper in nearby Clifford Chambers.

Jane Edwards's father may not have been as satisfied with the local police as the rest of the population (Jane Edwards being the woman who developed Mayfield Avenue). He called for the assistance of the local constable, in 1862, when he caused Ellen Blackford to be arrested for misdemeanour. He thought she had swindled him out of a pair of shoes that he had made. However, the court threw out his case, describing the action as 'disqualified... the evidence varying from the charge'. He was left with court costs of 10s 9d with two shillings added for the cost of calling the constable. He may well have been furious at the outcome - but at least he had a constable to call.

'The police question'

Trouble surfaced again in 1864 when Stratford responded strongly to the consolidation of the County and Borough forces. Regular reports featured in the *Herald* on what became known as 'The Police Question'.[47] Passions became focussed on a proposal to extend the police station in Sheep Street into the Rose and Crown. This was simply an expansion into next door but there was disproportionate and rowdy disagreement. Several acrimonious meetings later, with opinions sharply divided, a call went out to 'let well alone'. Jane Edward's father and husband were both signatories to a petition along with over three-hundred aldermen, town councillors and the Mayor.[48] It was sent to Warwick urging the County to cease its cost-cutting efforts and allow local people to manage their own affairs as it 'is most conducive to the general good'. But local opinion was ignored and eventually in 1866 work began on the move and Stratford gained a much improved police station.

More trouble occurred in 1866 when local JPs were again reluctant to comply with yet another County directive. This time it was about convenience and fairness: Warwick had directed that pre-trial prisoners be housed in cells on Guild Street in the Petty Session House instead of in the police station attached to the Town Hall. This meant that the constables had to escort prisoners half a mile through town from Guild Street to the Town Hall where the Borough sessions were heard. This caused problems for the constables and was felt to force unfair public exposure on those prisoners who might later be proved innocent. They wanted 'to carry on as before'.[49] The town dignitaries had a valid point but they lost - again.

If the politics behind the local police force involved acrimony and obtuseness, the policing of the streets had also become a troubled business. Under the command of Superintendent William Rawlings one constable had been accused of 'offering an untruth and being insubordinate' whilst a second came up before the magistrates for 'unlawfully obtaining a reward for apprehending a deserter'; a third,

Constable Rose, was suspended for 'being drunk and incapable'. The force at this time was not, it would seem, in a happy state.

Superintendent Thomas Rowley

Fig 17. Cartoon of Thomas Rowley c.1868 courtesy of Guy Winter

This was to dramatically change with the arrival of Mr Thomas Rowley in 1868. He set up home at 1 Sheep Street, the police station, next to the Town Hall, and remained there until his retirement. With his arrival compliance, obedience and doing things right became the order of the day. A cartoon (Fig 17) depicting a monument supposedly to be 'erected in the centre of Bromsgrove Market Place by public subscription' says a lot about him. The monument was to commemorate 'the joy experienced by the entire community of Bromsgrove at the departure of Thomas Rowley'. He came to Stratford to be the Superintendent in 1868 and three years later he was Chief of Police. In 1870 at a Petty Session hearing, he elicited an apology from Mr John Gibbs (possibly a local inn-keeper) for making statements calculated to affect 'his (Rowley's) private and personal position'. Right from the start Rowley required respect.

A great deal of Rowley's time was spent completing paperwork, either returning forms from Whitehall or preparing accounts and reports for the Watch Committee. He complied with his quarterly accounts and itemised every penny spent including the frequent cost of washing rugs for the use in cells, and at other times the poisoning of dogs, the hire of a tricycle and the 'keep of a horse'.[50]

Where Rowley really changed things was in the introduction of quarterly reports. Previously the police chief had presented his report book and charge book along with the constables' report books to the Watch Committee for inspection. Reports of incidents were written up on a daily basis with Constables Clarke and Moule repeatedly entering 'nothing to report' and would have made for tiresome reading. After Rowley's arrival the quarterly reports were factual and to the point. His very first report, dated 4th May 1868, begins, 'Gentlemen, I beg to report that during the last quarter no cases of much importance have occurred within the Borough'. [51] He then listed the fifteen cases: two cases of felony, two attempts to obtain money under false pretences, four vagrants apprehended, three cases of drunkenness and four cases of breach of the peace. He concluded 'I have further to report my full satisfaction of the men under my control'.

From such brief but to-the-point reports it is possible to see the nature of the crimes that Rowley was trying to prevent. Of the 174 cases pursued from 1868 to 1880, over 47% involved the arrest of drunks. If offences associated with drunkenness such as breach of the peace, assault, suspicious behaviour, bad language, damage and vagrancy are added then the figure becomes over 72%. Cases of bigamy, cruelty (to a horse), bill posting, attempted suicide and indecent exposure must have caused a stir when they happened. Stratford was hardly a hotbed of crime and violence.

But the town was shocked in 1886 with the violent death of PC Hines, a local man from Ingon just outside Stratford. Hines was murdered within sight of his home in Fenny Compton where he served his beat. People were horrified; the coroner's verdict was 'wilful murder against some person or persons unnamed'. Hines's funeral, held in Stratford, was well attended and policemen lined Bridge Street as the coffin made its way to Holy Trinity Church. His death left a young widow and three very young children. In line with a national directive the widow was awarded one year's pay of £67 12s 0d. There was much sympathy for the plight of the young family and a town collection was organised via the pages of the *Herald*, which had reported the progress of the case in great detail.[52]

In January 1888 and close to his retirement, Rowley thought his constables were getting a bit slack with their persistent 'nothing to report' entries in the *Route and Occurrence Ledger*.[53] On the cover in red ink he wrote 'All cases reported to the Police must be entered in this book and the police constable will not take it upon himself not to enter it because in his opinion it is frivolous.' His constables took his reproof seriously and observed his instruction with assiduous detail, reporting a complaint of Mr Mason's about boys chalking on his walls, and of Mr Canning who took exception to 'a number of children in the habit of congregating in front of my house and using bad language and otherwise offending me'. Damage to a tree in town was the last entry immediately prior to Rowley's retirement. Perhaps even he eventually tired of all the detail.

The Specials

It could be that Chief of Police Thomas Rowley's success, despite having just four constables, was down to his judicial use of 'specials'. These were ordinary men, living in town, who were recruited by the magistrates to back up the constables. It was an arrangement first used in the reign of Charles II in 1673 and, over the years, was modified to allow recruitment in peaceful times - it was no longer necessary to wait for a riot to recruit them. Specials could be sworn in if it was felt that there were insufficient constables to deal with the policing, and clearly, this is what Rowley and his four constables relied on. In 1872 for instance, he had two JPs swear in six additional Specials to deal with unruly labourers building a nearby railway line.

The number of specials recruited (for limited periods) reached an all-time high of over three hundred in 1880 in contrast with a mere 105 recruited in 1858, before Rowley's arrival. Mrs Jane Edward's brother George volunteered in 1874 and her son-in-law Mr Thomas Olney in 1882. Both were shop-keepers so there may have been a hint of self-interest, but this was not always the case. The six recruited to deal with the railway skirmishes of 1872 were a baker, a labourer, a basket maker, a shoe maker, a machinist and a porter. Specials were generally not considered to be real 'coppers' and were often a bit unreliable but, whatever their reputation with the public, Superintendent Rowley certainly approved of them and used them to good effect.

Thomas Rowley died aged seventy-eight in 1902 at home in 38 West Street, a modest part of town. Just before he retired in 1889, his pay was set at £2 8s 1d per week. This was not a high wage; Sir Robert Peel had insisted that the police be paid more than a labourer but less than a skilled worker. Rowley's photo, part of a collection, *Portraits of Stratford Personalities*, implies a man of considerable social standing in town. We can perhaps assume that over his very long service he generated good will and respect. If not, towards the end of his days he would surely have left Stratford for quiet anonymity elsewhere.

Over his long career Rowley had seen authority over Stratford Borough Police Force gradually change. His retirement in 1889 coincided with responsibility being transferred to the newly formed County Council.

Fig 18. The Stratford-on-Avon Division of the Warwickshire Constabulary 1910

A photo taken, in 1910, of the twenty-eight members of the Stratford on Avon Division (Fig 18) was probably taken in the yard to the rear of the Petty Session building. All a far cry from the days of Rowley and his predecessor's when one constable and three-night watchmen patrolled the streets of peaceful, if somewhat drunken, Stratford.

Chapter 11

Messrs Fetherston & Manton

During a September afternoon in 1809 at the White Lion Inn, Mr John Keen's precious land had been divided and sold at auction. His grandchildren had made a fine profit and were living far from Stratford. Change was about to accelerate because there was money to be made in building houses for rent. Those who bought the small plots close to Guild Street had that in mind and Great William Street (called 'intended road' at the auction) rapidly took shape. The successful bidders for the larger plots, further into the fields, and where Mayfield Avenue was to appear, could afford to wait for the road to be extended. Mr John Fetherston who had bought Lots 11 and 13 did this; Mr John Manton, who bought Lot 14, was not so patient.

Documents of the time describe Mr Fetherston as a 'victualler', a person selling food and drink. He was the owner of a thriving pub, The Horseshoe, situated in Swine Street (now called The Queens Head on Ely Street Fig 2 No. 6). The inn had only recently become Fetherston's following the death of his father, William, in 1807. William had run the inn successfully as a tenant landlord for many years, until in 1805 when he paid £200 to a Mr Thomas Mason for the freehold. Two years after acquiring the freehold, William died and John, his only son, inherited The Horseshoe. It seems that John, like his father, had good business sense because he too became a wealthy man. Documents frequently describe him as a 'yeoman'. There were times when he was able to lease out the daily running of the pub to tenants and presumably take his ease elsewhere.

Over the years Mr Fetherston had bought land, leased it out and thereby gained an income. The purchase of Lots 11 and 13 was a speculative investment made attractive by the intended road and the presence of clay. The town was expanding rapidly and to have a ready supply of local clay for the bricks was a bonus. But there was possibly something else fuelling interest in the site. Although the canal would not open for another seven years it had been given the go-ahead back in 1793 and its course mapped out. It was going to curl round this side of town and at the time of the auction, it was well on the way to completion despite previous problems with funding. The notion that the area would benefit because of this new venture was correct, and Fetherston seems to have believed this.

A 'Great Rascal'

Mr Fetherston gained a good living from the Horseshoe and from his investments, as is demonstrated by his 1820 entry in the *Poll Register* which lists only the wealthy 'Freeholders of Warwickshire'.[54] However pencilled entries in the margin, which usually read 'dead' or 'left', has 'no vote' by his name. He may have lost his right to vote because of a previous crime and repeated contempt of court . He had been called to appear at the Warwickshire Quarter Sessions on 15th October 1816 because he (and a Mr Thomas Reeves Hobbins) had failed to appear at a hearing the previous year. The charge was that they 'unlawfully, unjustly and extorsively did exact take and receive of and from Christopher Parkinson the sum of ten pounds'.[55] The definition of extorsively at the time involved 'violence'. Both men had chosen once again to ignore the summons. It is probable that Mr Fetherston was deprived of the vote as a punishment for his act of 'felony', which was permissible at the time. He had also crossed the path of authority in 1817 when he was called before the Borough Court. He was accused by a Mr John Carloss, of Coventry, along with three other victuallers, of selling short measures of ale, it being 'otherwise thereby a full Ale pint according to the Standard of the exchequer'.[56] All four landlords were fined forty shillings each. Pencilled on the cover of the court document someone wrote: 'a great rascal' for he 'never came for summons'. Fetherston had failed to attend yet again. A contemporary definition of 'rascal' as a scoundrel, a villain, a sorry wretch is altogether more condemnatory than today's definition. He was rich and possibly arrogant and, it seems, quite a rough diamond. More of this later.

Having already acquired Lots 11 and 13 Mr Fetherston went on to buy Lot 14 from Mr Manton in early 1813 (Fetherston thereby became the sole owner of all the land that was to become associated with Mayfield Avenue). A year after buying the land at auction, Mr Manton had taken out a £300 loan with Mr William Stephens, a local farmer, and with this money he had developed the land quite extensively, building a cottage close to the new road and a brick kiln further to the west. By selling it on for £480 to Mr Fetherston, Manton paid off his loan and hopefully made a profit.

On the 27th October 1813 Fetherston did something rather odd with his newly acquired land and cottage. Rather surprisingly, he sold it to Mr George Edwards, a brick maker, for £650. Two men, Mr Thomas Cresswell and Mr John Perry, were involved when they facilitated the transaction, including the loans. The property was put up for auction yet again, at the Golden Lion Inn on Tuesday 3rd May 1814, less than a year later. During the intervening months Edwards had knocked down the existing cottage and built a new one, 'Elm Cottage' (now called 'Regency Cottage') siding onto the newly built Maidenhead Road. He also removed the brick kiln and created a garden. At auction Fetherston was the highest bidder, paying £650 for what, in effect, was the return of his own much improved land and property. This convoluted business, amongst men who knew each other very well, may have enabled a land-tax dodge.

If all the above sounds complicated - it was. In all the land-purchase transactions concerning the Mayfield land that follow down the years, there were always people providing cash in the form of loans, hoping for a profit via the interest charged. The loans would often roll on for years and sometimes people died before repayment. If that was the case, the agreement was inherited and perhaps re-negotiated or sometimes simply sold on to someone who thought they saw a good proposition. In the meanwhile, in 1819, Fetherston needed more money and borrowed £300 from Mr William Woods Weston using his Mayfield land as security.

By 1825 he was defined as a 'yeoman', not a victualler. Perhaps he was seeking to retire completely. In 1824 he had experienced a nasty run-in with his neighbours and was obliged to issue a complaint of assault.[57] 'Children had been in the habit of coming into his yard for water' and he objected to it. One evening, he told them off then 'pushed them down the alley' when they refused to leave. The mother of one, Elizabeth Pargiter, 'wife of Thomas Pargiter', and Mary Hewins, a 'single woman' 'came over and pushed and pulled and collared and otherwise assaulted' him. It must have come as a shock to Mr Fetherston to encounter these two formidable women from two formidable families. The dispute went before the mayor the next day but alas we don't know the outcome. It had certainly been an unpleasant experience and may have prompted Fetherston to give up his trade and leave the area. In the same year as his brush with Mrs Pargiter he leased 'The Horseshoe' to Mr Hyatt, who renamed it 'The New Bear'. Mr Hyatt and his wife were not only crooked but also incompetent and they were gone by 1829 when Fetherston sold the freehold to Mr Richard Tennett for £700.

Mr Fetherston could shed his pub, his main source of income, because he had already acquired money from the sale of his land. He had sold Lots 11 and 13 in 1825. The area was by then, with the opening of the canal, an even more attractive spot for developers. The town was described in a contemporary directory as 'likely to become a busy and thriving little port'. He chose not to go to auction but instead simply sold to Mr Richard Newland senior, a saddler, who paid him £605. On the back of the mortgage document where interested parties sign, there is the following: 'they do sell release and quit unto said Richard Newland and his heirs two several plots totalling 5 acres 0 rod 13 perch being Lots 11 and 13 agrees to pay £605'.[58] Of the £605, £300 went to Mr Woods Weston whilst £305 went to Mr Fetherston. In this way Fetherston was able to pay back his 1819 loan.

Two years later, in 1827, he sold Lot 14. This sale was probably also conducted by word of mouth since once again no auction was involved. Mr Abraham Newland junior stepped up to buy, not for himself but for his sister Mary 'to whom the premises must be conveyed'. Lawyers were brought in to clarify the right of Mrs Martha Fetherston, John's wife, to dower in or out of the property subsequent to her husband's death (*see* Chapter 5). They must have been satisfied because the sale went ahead for £610. Two years later Mr Fetherston sold The New Bear and by 1831 had 'retired' and ten years later was nowhere in town.

Chapter 12

The Workhouse

By leaving the town when he did Mr Fetherston did not witness the opening of the new, huge Union Workhouse. Over the years Stratford had two workhouses. The first was a small affair located in a converted cottage in Henley Street. Its successor, the Union Workhouse, was a huge and formidable institution dominating Arden Street. Its dark bulk would have loomed over the poor, who aimed to keep clear of it, while the rich saw it as a social and economic necessity.

The Union Workhouse was the unfortunate product of rising concern about the increasing cost of out-relief for the destitute (support given with the recipient pauper remaining in the community). This was not a new problem; parishes had struggled with the burden of keeping their indigent poor ever since the dissolution of the monasteries and the subsequent loss of the free care they had provided. Various laws had been passed to deal with the inconvenient destitute poor. In 1536 it became illegal to give alms to 'roaming beggars' because it was seen to encourage them. The Poor Rate was introduced in 1572 and henceforth the well-off were obliged to pay a sum towards relief of the destitute. Overseers were elected at Vestry meetings to manage the whole business and, in this way, out-relief remained closely linked to the church's authority. The 1662 Settlement Laws with their Settlement Certificates did little to improve matters.

By 1722 parishes were able to set up institutions called workhouses in order to reduce the incidence of out-relief and by 1725 Stratford had the Corporation Workhouse on the corner of Henley Street with Windsor Street (Fig 2 No. 30). Later, via the Thomas Gilbert Act of 1782, neighbouring parishes were allowed to unite their efforts in order to make further savings. In theory the workhouses were only for the sick, orphans and the old - the deserving poor; able-bodied paupers were to be found work outside and their wages supplemented from the poor rates. The Speenham System, set up in 1795, had a sliding scale of means-tested top-up payments to supplement low wages but had the unfortunate effect of lowering wages thus causing even more hardship. It was also thought to breed laziness. All so-called solutions to the problem of increasing costs seemed only to make matters worse.

Following a royal commission in 1832, it was decided that larger workhouses would be more economical and would answer the problems created by previous attempts at reform. With the passing of the 1834 Poor Law Amendment Act the somewhat homely Corporation Workhouse was closed to make way for the Union Workhouse on Arden Street. The underlining principle was that out-relief for the able-bodied was to cease and relief was to be only for those unable to work. The able bodied, when destitute, were to receive relief via work, hard work, and that work was to take place *within* the workhouse. Life for able-bodied inmates was to be harsh, worse than the prevailing conditions for the poor on the outside so as to discourage malingering. The paupers must earn their meagre food-rations by working at unpleasant tasks such as stone breaking, oakum-picking and wool-picking. The unhappy paupers who sought shelter within the workhouse walls were thought to be feckless and lazy and had only themselves to blame.

The Corporation Workhouse

Before this momentous change was implemented the Corporation Workhouse had served its purpose reasonably well. The building dated back to 1473 and was, for a long time, just four or five tenements. It was situated on the corner of Henley Street opposite the White Lion Inn (Fig 19). The 1765 smallpox census records a total of thirty people living there.

Poor Law overseers made sure it was run as cheaply as possible, thereby keeping the Poor Rate down. An effective way to reduce costs was to send young inmates to live in the community as pauper-apprentices. In 1762 Mr Payton took on Noble Haywood as such in his smart White Lion Inn, to be trained in husbandry until he reached the age of twenty-one. He had to provide him with 'a good new suit for the Holy Day and another for the Working Day' along with 'sufficient Meat, Drink and Apparel, Lodging, Washing and all other Things necessary'.

Fig 19. The Corporation workhouse c.1835

In 1792 and 1794, a drastic strategy was employed to reduce the number of young poor who may in the future have recourse to the workhouse. Thirty-two children were sent to the mills of Mr Joseph Wilkes of Measham, Derby to be calico/cotton apprentices.[59] They were to stay there until they married or reached the age of twenty-one. The youngest was just seven years old and the oldest fourteen-and-a-half. They were children of destitute families, of widows or they were rejected bastards. The initiative did not run smoothly and there were 'ugly rumours circulating' of cruelty. Some of the children absconded and a thirteen-year-old, Thomas Smith, was apparently so injured that he had his hand amputated in Birmingham Hospital. Two overseers of the workhouse were sent to investigate conditions at Measham. The children were gathered in a room and the mill supervisors were told to leave so that the children could speak freely. Back in Stratford the overseers reported that 'Few complaints were made of a trivial nature as to be unworthy of notice'. After further investigation, it was discovered that the injury had been inflicted on poor Thomas by his own father and he had been further battered when he was hit by a 'brick-bat' thrown by his sister. He had not 'dared to tell the truth as he thought his father would kill him'.

When Mr and Mrs Rutter sent their two children, Nancy and Thomas to the mill they perhaps believed that they were sending them away from the poverty of Stratford and to a better life. This kind of transportation of cheap child labour, dire though it was, proved not too disastrous for some. Their son Thomas became a weaver in Measham, married a local woman, had six children and lived to be eighty-two. He had a hard life but it was one with a wage, something that was not always guaranteed in rural Warwickshire.

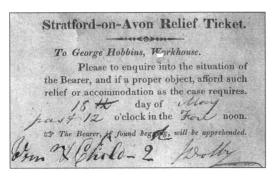

Fig 20. Ticket to the workhouse 1824

Admittance to the workhouse came via a written referral from a workhouse overseer. Mr Dolby, a tailor, became an overseer in 1824 and at first used simple hand-written notes for his referrals. Later the whole process became more formal and printed tickets were used. One of his tickets refers to a woman and her child and includes the strict instruction not to beg in the meanwhile (Fig 20).

The 1831census showed a total of fifty-four inmates with George and Hannah Hobbins as the master and matron. Resident paupers were fed and when fit they worked. Only those inmates deemed 'too ill, insane, blind or an idiot' were exempt from working. Inmates were sent out into the town to weed and sweep the streets or to work in people's homes and they were allowed to keep a few pennies for themselves from the proceeds of their labour.[60] Arnold Thomas, aged fifty-seven, worked periodically for the town's 'surveyor' and in doing so earned good money for the workhouse. Young William Napp, just nine-years-old when he entered the workhouse, was at first allowed to attend school but when he turned ten his attendance at school became patchy because he was required to work at the local brickworks, weed the streets or pick wool. A day's work at the brick yard brought in two shillings for the workhouse and, of that William was allowed to keep two pence. By the time he was eleven he was stone-breaking and school was a thing of the past. Girls fared a little better. When not sweeping the streets they were 'knitting for the house'. The elderly supported 'the house' by cooking, cleaning, tailoring, sewing, gardening, cobbling or 'spinning mops for sale'. The efforts of the inmates kept costs down and the running of the workhouse generally met with public approval.

The Union Workhouse

The Poor Law Amendment Act of 1834, spelled out a more brutal method for dealing with the destitute. Under its directives, the destitute of thirty-six surrounding parishes were corralled together and the small workhouse on Henley Street closed. The land required was purchased in 1836 and plans for a huge institution drawn up. It was to be built in fields off Arden Street, to the north of town (Fig 2 No. 39). The initial cost was £4,380 with a further £1,064 needed later. With this level of investment it had to pay for itself. Given a national increase in non-conformist church membership, management of the new institutions was to be via elected Boards of Governors. The national rules and regulations stipulated how these monstrous places were to be run. Stratford was to have a total of forty-four 'Guardians', at least one from each of the thirty-seven contributing parishes. Hopefully they were all well aware of their duties by the time Stratford's 'directions,' dated 25th January 1838, arrived from London.[61] These stated that all was to be 'in place by 9th February next' and certainly by April 1839 the first master was well established in his new role.

Using the census and the local archives it is possible to trace approximately ninety years of workhouse activity. For nearly seventy of those years just four masters and matrons (always married couples) ruled this small, desperate world. The first of the four were Thomas and Lucy Salmon who remained in post for over thirty years. Then Richard and Susan Bagley, Charles and Elizabeth Collingwood and finally the last master and matron, Daniel and Eleanor Pickett. The master's role was clearly defined in the regulations. He was to ensure that inmates worked hard, were punctual and never questioned the routine. The matron had to ensure that all paupers were given clean stockings and linen each week and that their sheets were changed monthly. Cleanliness was her main preoccupation, with fresh air and good ventilation a close second. The teacher's, the porter's and the medical officer's duties were similarly defined. To the master fell the additional task of attending court to explain paupers' deaths, and he did this with great regularity.

The rules and regulations were clear and detailed about who could admit a pauper. Leaving was a simpler matter: an inmate had to give three hours' notice and their leaving was then recorded as 'own request'. This was the preferred route and was taken as soon as possible by those who could. However, many inmates left by dying and others went mad and were sent to the county asylum.

On being admitted the new inmate was examined by the medical officer. If they were sick they went to the sick ward and if 'lunatic' to the 'lunatics' and idiots' ward'. If they were neither sick nor lunatic, they went to the area of their 'class' or type but before that they were cleaned and children had their hair cut. Meanwhile their clothes were 'removed, purified and stored'. Thereafter everyone wore the workhouse uniform. The seven different classes of inmate were:

1. Aged and infirm men
2. Able bodied men over 13
3. Youth and boys 7-13
4. Aged and infirm women
5. Able-bodied women and girls over 16
6. Girls 7 and under 16
7. Children under 7

They were to be kept strictly apart. The exceptions were mothers in class five who could have 'reasonable contact' with their children in class seven, whilst class one and four could be together if married.

Discipline and routine were the overriding preoccupations. All inmates had to rise with the bell in silence and eat in silence. Grace was said before meals and additional prayers read twice a day. Children had three hours of education a day which involved reading, writing and the Christian religion 'in order that they become virtuous'. Disorderly conduct such as 'swearing, not washing, pretending to be sick or refusing an order' was punishable by being 'placed in an apartment provided for such offences' and with an 'alteration to their diet'. Truly bad behaviour, defined as 'refractory', brought the same punishment but was followed by an appearance before a JP. William Mitchell - after 'he did wilfully destroy his own clothes, contrary to the Paupers, Inmates Discharge and Regulation Act 1870'- was sentenced by a JP to three months in prison with hard labour.

The whole system relied on close attention to the numbers involved. A pauper's arrival was logged in the Admissions Register and their leaving in the Discharge Register. When Charlotte Martin was recorded as 'discharged' on the 22nd April 1909, she was not off home but was on her way to Hatton asylum. Six other paupers who left on that day all discharged themselves despite being sick. They must have rated their chances better on the outside, which was just what the system was meant to encourage. The number of paupers was published weekly in the *Herald* and compared with the same week in the previous year. In this very public way the people of Stratford could see that their rates were being judiciously spent. In a typical week in 1873 there was a total of 143 resident paupers. This was thirty-three up on the same week the previous year, not good news at all.

If routine, hard work, cleanliness and godliness were important, so too was food. Meticulous counting ensured only the correct number of meals of the correct type were cooked. Any hungry Oliver requesting more would be refused. Meals were uniformly terrible with tea, butter and sugar only available to the over-sixties in lieu of gruel. Each meal was listed in the *Directory of Allowances for Paupers* (Fig 21).[62]

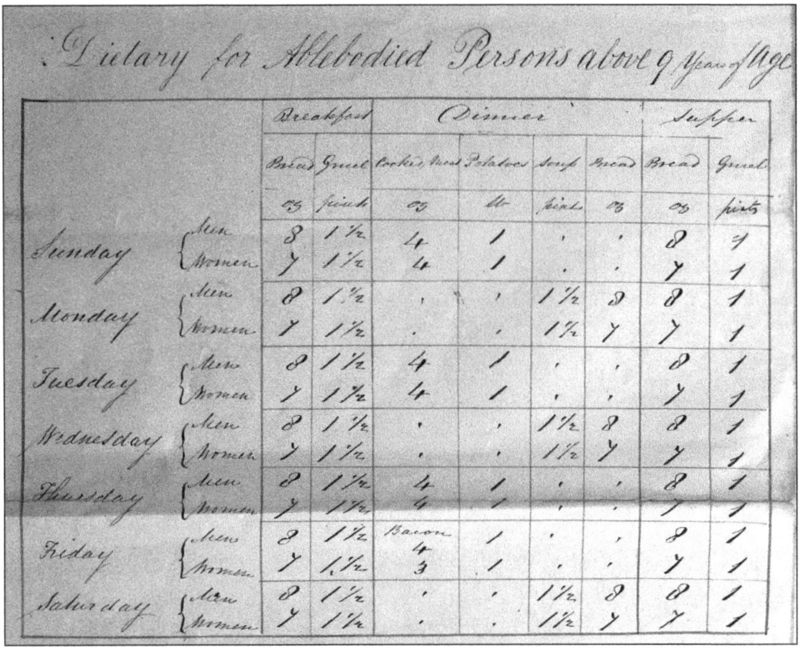

Dietary for Ablebodied Persons above 9 Years of Age			Breakfast		Dinner					Supper	
			Bread	Gruel	Cooked Meat	Bread	Potatoes	Soup	Bread	Bread	Gruel
			oz	pint	oz	lb	pint	oz	oz	pints
Sunday	Men		8	1½	4	1	·	·	8	1
	Women		7	1½	4	1	·	·	7	1
Monday	Men		8	1½	·	·	1½	2	8	1
	Women		7	1½	·	·	1½	7	7	1
Tuesday	Men		8	1½	4	1	·	·	8	1
	Women		7	1½	4	1	·	·	7	1
Wednesday	Men		8	1½	·	·	1½	2	8	1
	Women		7	1½	·	·	1½	7	7	1
Thursday	Men		8	1½	4	1	·	·	8	1
	Women		7	1½	4	1	·	·	7	1
Friday	Men		8	1½	Bacon 4	1	·	·	8	1
	Women		7	1½	3	1	·	·	7	1
Saturday	Men		8	1½	·	·	1½	8	8	1
	Women		7	1½	·	·	1½	7	7	1

Fig 21. The workhouse menu 1837

From reading the entries in the record books it is difficult to conclude who a typical pauper might be. The following three examples illustrate very different experiences leading to incarceration.

Fanny Payne, aged nineteen, was admitted in 1881 with her one-month-old baby. Ten years earlier Fanny had been living within a large family in Garrick Court, off Greenhill Street (Fig 2 No. 12), one of the squalid courts that were infamous at the time. She had five older brothers and sisters and was born when her mother was aged forty-two. Her father Joseph was 'a rough carpenter'. Having had the baby, she entered the workhouse. This was most likely a pragmatic decision driven by poverty rather than shame and would have been the route whereby the father could be chased for maintenance. Joseph and his wife, both in their early sixties, were probably unable to cope. Her mother, Mrs Payne, died in hospital three years later and was, perhaps, already in poor health. Fanny's initial admittance in 1881 was repeated several times in her short life. When not in the workhouse she earned her living as a char woman. She was last admitted in July 1894 and remained there for her last eight years when her departure, recorded as 'dead', on the 13th April 1902, aged just thirty-nine. The cause of her death was *morbus cordis*; her heart had simply given up. She was buried in the local cemetery and her plot is number 1354.

Alfred Bull's admissions spanned a period of many years but the pattern within those years was very different from Fanny's. He first stayed in 1893 for two months over Christmas. He returned a week later and stayed a further three months. He returned nearly ten years later, in September 1903, and remained, again over Christmas. He did the same more or less for Christmas 1904. Christmas inside, it seems, held an attraction for Alfred. He then disappeared returning in September 1907. In between these winter stop-overs he was sometimes in for a few days at a time, sometimes just for the night. From 1907 up to his final admission in 1908, he appeared on at least thirteen occasions. He was what became known as an 'in and out'. Was he a bit of a chancer or simply not coping well with life outside? He would have been seen as a vagrant and so, within the rules, he could not be turned away. Having completed an amount of stone-breaking he would have earned the right to stay and get a meal or two.

The Wesson children all found themselves in the workhouse in 1901. Alfred aged twenty, Albert nineteen, Florence seven, Constance five and William just one were incarcerated along with their eighty-one-year old grandma Sarah. They had been in three years earlier in 1898, at which time there had been two additional children, eleven-month Rose who had died in the workhouse and Violet Ann, who fared better because she was taken and 'put into service' in May 1900. For the mother, Mrs Wesson, having her surviving children return to the workhouse when she had already lost Rose there, must have been a hard blow. Usually when children were taken in it was to allow the father to work and the mother to recover from illness or repeated child birth. But the crisis in this family had been caused by the death of their father earlier in 1901. Since the older boys, who would have been in work, are included, it would seem that they had also lost their home. With her entire family in the workhouse Mrs Wesson was no doubt trying to recover her strength and work out how, as newly widowed with no income and no home, the family was to survive.

When a pauper died it was sometimes necessary to hold an inquiry or an inquest. On each occasion the master was required to give evidence – and the outcome was inevitably 'a visitation of God' and so nobody's fault. In 1839 the master, Mr Salmon, was required to attend the Coroner's Court for 'an inquisition on the body of Mr John Hodgkins', a staggeringly unlucky man.[63] Mr Salmon told the court that the deceased had been in the workhouse 'since last Thursday and is 59 years of age'. Having had the usual dinner he noticed that Hodgkins was sick and removed some meat from his throat and called for the medical officer, 'but he died before he came'. The medical officer, Mr Burman, said that when he arrived the deceased 'was quite dead' and that he had 'found a large piece of gristle in the throat and have no doubt that the man died of choking'. Mr Burman described how when Mr Hodgkins came to the workhouse he complained that he was destitute, but he had 'found upon him a shilling and parts of a loaf of bread'. Mr Burman added that Hodgkins wished to come into the workhouse 'on account of the ill-treatment he received from his wife'. The verdict: 'that the said Hodgkins died on the 7th of July by the visitation of God'. Death was caused by 'choking and suffocating and not by any violent means whatsoever to the knowledge of the said jurors'. Cost to the court £2 5s 6d.

The Children

The 1833 and 1844 Factory Acts had made the provision of education a duty for commercial employers and the Stratford workhouse, which was an employer after a fashion, followed this requirement by employing a teacher. One, Miss Ann Clarke, sued for libel in 1877 when her cruelty was exposed by the rather naïve workhouse chaplain. He accused her of beating a ten-year-old with 'all her strength so that he howled'.[64] She did not leave quietly and her anger was reported in the *Herald*. The Guardians response was fortunately positive: they decided to send the pauper children, nineteen girls and thirteen boys, to the local National Schools on Alcester Road, safely away from Miss Clarke. Nationally the whole business of having children in workhouses was a subject of concern. Why should they suffer because of the actions of their parents? Back in 1839 it was recorded that nationally 50% of inmates were children and that figure was reflected in Stratford.

In 1881, the *Herald* reported the number of inmates had reached a peak of seventy-four, which included many children, and concluded that a cycle of dependency was developing. To stop this, children would be 'boarded out' giving them sight of a better life. The Boarding Out Committee was in reality providing cheap labour. One prospective employer even failed to set aside a place for the child to sleep, a basic right that should never have been overlooked. An attempt to correct things was made by the 1908 Children's Act, which gave local authorities additional powers to keep children out of the workhouse. It had an effect in Stratford; by 1911 children under ten represented just 10% of the inmate population and in 1915 the Guardians bought a house in Wellesbourne where the pauper children could live a more homely life.

By 1911 Mr Pickett, was in charge of 164 inmates (and 63 'casuals'), a high proportion being old and sick.[65] The matron now had an assistant, a nurse and three 'sick' nurses to assist her, reflecting the increased health needs of her elderly residents. The workhouse was gradually becoming a home for the elderly and less like something out of a Dickens novel. On 15th January 1915, Mr Pickett reported in the *Herald* that the inmates enjoyed a very good Christmas due to a large number of gifts. He said, 'those inside had had a better time than a good many outside'. The Union Workhouse officially ceased to function at midnight on the 31st March 1930. This was when the new Public Assistance Boards took over and it became a 'public assistance institution' run by the local authority. The term 'pauper' gave way to 'resident', uniforms were abandoned and residents were free to come and go. The address was now simply 50 Arden Street. Finally the 1948 National Assistance Act ensured that the workhouse was completely merged with the hospital next door.

Maria Coggins

For many paupers when life was a struggle, a fragile affair, the workhouse could be crucial to survival. Maria Coggins' life illustrates the part the workhouse could play when times were hard and unexpected events threw life into crisis. Her parents, Elizabeth and John Coggins, lived in 10 Great William Street (Fig 2 No. 35) with their children Anne, Elizabeth, Jabez, Jane and Alfred. Maria was born early in 1847 but John, her father, had died the previous November of 'gastric fever' and 'congestion of the lungs' (probably typhoid). He had been a shoe maker and the sole bread-winner which meant that Elizabeth was suddenly a widow with six children and no income. Elizabeth experienced a double tragedy: the church burial records show that that same year on 26th December, a month after her husband's death, her four-year old-son, Alfred, was also buried. He may well have succumbed to the same infection.

Life became exceedingly harsh for Elizabeth. By 1851, when Maria was a three-year-old, her sisters Ann and Elizabeth had left home, probably to go into service. Elizabeth raised an income by being 'a private schoolmistress' and she continued to do this over the years. Great William Street was very different from the car-crowded strip it is today. At that time it was a relatively isolated spur of houses jutting into fields, and perhaps the only thing in its favour was that it was certainly not as crowded and unhealthy as the courts in the centre of town. Most residents were poor and in low-paid work and large families were the norm. From the age of nine upwards most children were at work on the nearby canal or in the local brickworks. In 1857 Maria's mother, Elizabeth, married Richard Dunn, an older widower. He was an illiterate agricultural worker and the family went to live in his house in Alveston, just outside Stratford.

In early 1870 Elizabeth died, aged fifty-eight when Maria was twenty-two. Maria continued to live with her seventy-four-year old step-father. Six years after her mother's death, at the age of twenty-eight, she was admitted into the workhouse 'for her own safety' - and categorised as 'an imbecile from birth'.[66] Once there, things could only get worse. Just a few months after her admission, Dr James Johnstone, the workhouse doctor, found her to be 'in a low, nervous, desponding state approaching closely to melancholia; at times refusing to take food for two to three days consecutively and altogether keeps in a miserable dejected condition'. According to the matron and nurse at the workhouse, 'the patient of late has been very troublesome and frequently absconding from the house, on one occasion being remonstrated by one of the other patients in the ward, threw a stick at her and afterwards attempted to stick her with the poker'. Because of this one violent act she was committed to the local asylum. Mr Arthur Hodgton, the magistrate presiding at her hearing, signed the order for committal to Warwickshire County Lunatic Asylum (later known as Hatton Asylum) on the 27th June 1876.

Dr Henry Parsey was in charge there and Maria was committed to his care on the 30th June 1876. The paperwork for the 'Reception of a Pauper Patient' tells us a great deal. Once admitted to the asylum, her patient record, No. 2582, speaks more kindly of her despite defining her as 'a congenital idiot'. When assessing her capabilities they found that she 'displays a fair amount of intelligence'. She could read and write 'fairly well', multiply by units of two, use a 'needle well' and was 'capable of doing light housework' although 'she seldom speaks unless spoken to'. The rebellious spirit, exhibited in the workhouse with the poker, appears to have deserted her. Four years later, in July 1880, it was noted that there had been no change to 'this quiet soul' and so on 28th August she was discharged.

If Maria was too sane for the asylum, she was nowhere near savvy enough for the streets of Stratford and life at home. Following her release she was repeatedly brought back into the workhouse. There were to be at least five more admissions, the final one on September 18th

1886, six years after her release from the asylum. This was prompted by the death of her ninety-year-old step-father just five months earlier in April. It seems that Richard tried his best to look after her but when it all got too much, Maria would be admitted for a while. With him gone, she stayed in the workhouse until she was discharged 'dead' on the 16th September 1907 (Fig 22). [67]

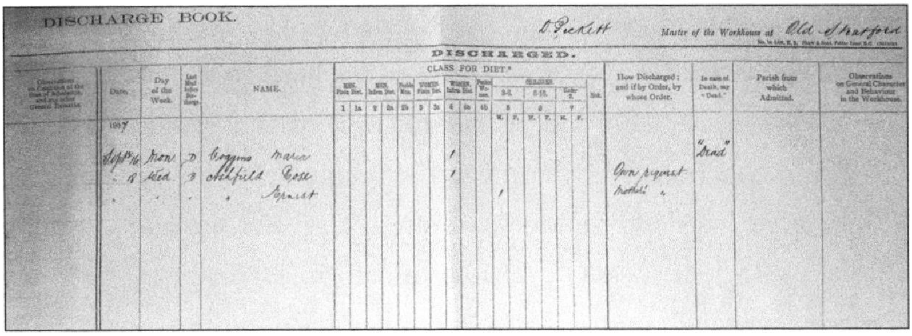
DISCHARGE BOOK.

Master of the Workhouse at Old Stratford

DISCHARGED.

Date.	Day of the Week.	NAME.	How Discharged; and if by Order, by whose Order.	In case of Death, say "Dead."
1907				
Sept 16	Mon	Coggins Maria		"Dead"

Fig 22. Maria Coggins' final leaving 1907

As usual, no cause of death was given on the register but her death certificate states *Cerebral Softening.* She was fifty-nine and had remained there for her last twenty-one years. The place of death was 50 Arden Street - the workhouse. Her grave in the cemetery is No. 2114.

Chapter 13

The Newland Team

The Newlands, the next owners of the Mayfield Avenue land, were a far cry from the previous owner John Fetherston. He was a rather dubious character who ran a profitable pub on Ely Street in one of the roughest parts of town; the Newlands lived above their shop at 27, Bridge Street (Fig 2 No. 21) where Richard Newland senior and his two sons, Richard and Abraham, worked as saddlers. Mary, his wife, and daughters Mary and Elizabeth completed the family.

Richard Newland senior was more than just a successful saddler; he had sufficient means to enable him to invest in property. When he wrote his will, on the 29th September 1826, he was very clear as to how it should be shared. His wife Mary would live off the income from an investment of £1,400 so long 'as she continues my widow and unmarried'. The Bridge Street shop was to go to the eldest son, Richard, along with the two cottages at the 'bottom of the garden' plus the 'garden in Guild Pitts'. His other properties were to be shared between the four children 'to share and share alike' as tenants in common, which included the 'close of five acres in Maidenhead Road' that he had purchased just a year earlier from Mr Fetherston. He died, in 1827, shortly after making this will.

The four Newland children inherited the Mayfield Avenue land, Lots 11 and 13, and meanwhile, and in the same year that his father died and probably with cash that he had inherited, Richard bought Lot 14 from Mr Fetherston - in his sister Mary's name. All the Mayfield Avenue land was once again owned by a group of siblings - one thinks back to the Morris family. However, the Newlands steered an entirely different course and their subsequent deaths brought benefit, not confusion.

Following the death of their mother the remaining family wealth went to the four siblings: Richard, Abraham, Mary and Elizabeth. They all remained unmarried, and for a while were very much alive and living quietly together at 27 Bridge Street, then called Back Bridge Street (Fig 23 to the left of Middle Row looking towards the river). The brothers played an active part in civic matters and were called in to be 'specials' during the 1832 riot (*see* Chapter 4). Richard was the town auditor in 1830 and was sworn in as a Borough councillor in 1836. Abraham was the Borough's assessor in 1840 and one brother was a workhouse overseer. It is difficult not to conclude that the Newlands were really rather a nice bunch.

Fig 23. Back Bridge Street c.1858

A rude interruption to their quiet lives had occurred back in 1821. Emma Wilkins lived in nearby Kineton. A single woman, she became pregnant and cited Richard, then thirty, as the father of her baby, a scandal that must have set tongues wagging in the town. On the 12th June, the details were written down, under oath, on a small sheet of plain paper headed 'An examination of Emma Wilkins in a Case of Bastardy'.[68] The record was made by Mr Elias Webb, a JP, who added, 'that said child is likely to be born a bastard and to be chargeable to the Parish of Kineton' and 'Richard Newland is the father'. Emma signed it. It would appear that she was not expecting Richard to step up and marry her and the main concern, at this point, was the cost of such a child to the parish. Richard's character does not seem to have been unduly besmirched and he went on to become a pillar of the community.

In 1834, the second Newland son, Abraham, was persuaded by a Mr James Ward to invest £490 in his new 'ventilator' patent application. He entered into a contract whereby Ward agreed to pay a 'moiety' (half share) to Abraham of any profits. Repayments were not forthcoming even though the 'ventilator' proved profitable. A successful court order required Ward to show his accounts every six months and to hand over 50% of the profit until the debt was paid. By 1846 they had dissolved the painful partnership and went their separate ways. In 1838 and 1839 Abraham financed two plots of land, on Clopton Street (*see* Chapter 17). This part of town was rapidly expanding and must have seemed a sound investment and a far safer place for surplus money than new-fangled inventions. Apart from these two incidents the lives of the Newlands were for the most part uneventful and no doubt closely tied to their Christian values.

Inherited wealth

The Newlands' interest in buying land or lending money to builders came about because they had not only inherited their father's property and money, but also additional money from two aunts. These were Elizabeth Parsons, a spinster, and Dorothy Smith, a widow, both sisters of their late mother Mary. With the death of these women the accumulated wealth went to the four Newland children. Richard and his brother Abraham did rather better than Elizabeth and Mary because they inherited Aunt Elizabeth's property near to the post office in Henley Street whilst Mary and Elizabeth received her clothes. The rest of the estate was sold and the money divided equally between all four. The four Newland children had become very rich by inheritance, owning property around Stratford, Studley, Willicote, Beaudeset, Leamington and Shottery.

If their wealth came via the death of elderly relatives, the question of their own deaths could not be ignored. Who was to benefit when they, as unmarried middle-aged adults, died? The answer to that question was quite unusual and happened sooner than expected because three of the four Newlands were soon to die, the first just eleven short years after inheriting their dead relative's money.

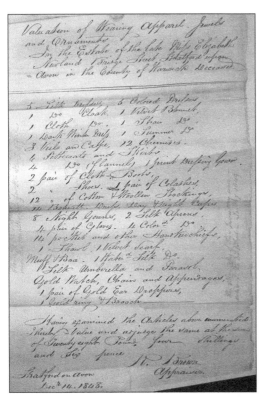

Fig 24. Inventory of Elizabeth Newland's wardrobe 1848

The first Newland sibling to die was Elizabeth, in April 1848 aged just forty-two. Not having written a will, Letters of Administration were granted from the Court of the Archbishop of Canterbury on 17th December of that year. Her property consisted of shares in the canal, and mortgages owing to her, amounting to £2,665. All went to her brother Richard. Her personal property was subject to evaluation and an inventory was compiled that listed her clothing, right down to her stockings (Fig 24). Including her gold jewellery, the total value came to £28 4s 6d. [69]

Abraham was the next to die, four years later, aged fifty-six. He wrote his will on the 13th August 1852 and died less than a month later. The will was proved in the Court of Canterbury on the 7th July 1853. Apart from the shared property, he also had his own property worth £9,000. This he left to Richard and Mary as tenants in common.

Life must have become quite worrying for Mary because Richard wrote his will on the 12th September 1854 and was dead within three months, aged sixty-three. The will was proved via the Court of

Canterbury in February the following year. However he left everything to her and an inventory of his personal property was prepared on his death.[70] Unlike his sister Elizabeth's inventory, his underwear and shoes were not counted but everything in the Bridge Street house, along with the farm he owned at August Hill, was. The amount of furniture filling the house was remarkable and the auditor listed everything right down to the nut-crackers and fourteen 'custard cups'.

With the death of Richard, Mary had lost her entire immediate family in the space of just six years. She was as a result, and as a kind of consolation, a very rich spinster in sole control of great wealth. The death of Richard must have prompted her to think very carefully about what she wanted to do. Any pondering was brief because by 1855, less than a year after Richard's death, she gave £500 to the Infirmary to bail it out of a financial mess. In today's money this sum would be about £60,000. And that was just the beginning. By 1857, barely three years later, she had already set the wheels of an ambitious plan in motion, and an essential part of that plan entailed writing her will, which might have been a worrying thing to do. She wrote it on the 24th November 1857 and in it she left all her estate to William Warrilow and William Gibbs in trust for sale. As things turned out, she did not die immediately but lived on to reach the age of seventy, dying on the 14th February 1866, leaving a legacy that is with us today.

Mary was determined that her wealth should be put to good use. In particular she wanted it to benefit four poor spinsters and widows by providing them with secure accommodation and income for the rest of their lives. The way to do that was to initially build four cottages. Importantly, she was determined they would benefit from her wealth *before* she died. Her brothers had demonstrated a social conscience by becoming involved with civic affairs. Now was the time for her to show her concern and in a way that was socially acceptable. She wasted no time and by 1857 had built the cottages on Guild Street behind the family business (Fig 2 No. 22) on land inherited from her brother. Her dream was going to happen within her lifetime, with her say-so and soon.

Mary's thinking is made clear in a simple note written on the 12th June 1857. This note explains that having 'pulled down a barn' she had built 'four substantial cottages'.[71] They were to be 'endowed with the sum of £2,400', the interest from which was to cover weekly payments to the four residents who were to be 'four poor and respectable widows or spinsters resident in the Borough or Parish of Stratford'. The trustees, the vicar and church wardens, were to take on the role 'for the time being'. It all seemed simple and straight forward, but things became increasingly complicated and fraught due to a recent change in the law governing such charitable actions. Mr Kemp, an expert, was called to advise. He stated that Miss Newland might object to the idea of the trustees taking over the management of her trust and 'care was needed' in telling her this, but, she would have to comply. On the 17th September 1857 she gave written instructions to 'prepare deeds' but on the 13th October, 1857, she was required to hand over the four cottages to the vicar and seven other trustees as per the new law, which she did reluctantly.

In order for the residents to have a secure future Mary needed to safeguard the long-term funding. The £2,400 already set aside was increased by a further £227, to be invested for 'repairs and rates' with any excess paid to the occupants. It can be seen that she wanted the interest, generated from investment, to go to the residents with nothing put aside. In 1860, she issued a large number of 'notices to quit' to her tenants in properties scattered round town. By selling these she was able to raise sufficient income to ensure the future finances of her four cottages and their residents.

The first occupants were Mary Cooper, Elizabeth Calloway, Mary Hewins and, surprisingly, Thomas Mayneod. Thomas was a married man, a shoemaker who had lived on Waterside. Why was he included, along with his wife and nephew? A mystery. He was to remain resident for thirteen years until his death in 1870.

Over the years, detailed ledgers were kept, recording the names of the residents and how the money was spent.[72] Although the spinsters and widows were able to live 'rent free for the rest of their lives', this was conditional on 'good behaviour'. The condition was differently described over the years, at one time not being found guilty of 'disgraceful or disorderly conduct' was thought sufficient. Fig 25 shows two residents, probably Ann Hobbins and Mary Knight who were residents during the 1911 census. Additional money which had been invested over the years went to the benefit of the poor of Stratford, providing an annual gift of coal, distributed in quantities of 1 and 2 cwt. Also £20 was shared equally between 'ten poor men and ten poor women'. These donations continued until 1945.

Fig 25. Mary Newland's alms-houses c.1910

Mary Newland lived until 1866 and although she did not have hands-on control as she had initially wanted, nevertheless she saw the alms houses fulfilling her original plan. Her death and the money raised by the auction of the remainder of her property more than ensured that the trust continued down the years. The houses she had built can be seen on Guild Street and are known as 'Guild Cottages'. They still observe the same rules as those first set out by Mary and are managed by the Municipal Charities.

Mary Newland was a very rich woman indeed. Even after her benevolent work she still had plenty of money to spare. The paperwork generated by her solicitors, Slatter Son & More, following her death was considerable because Mary named at least sixty beneficiaries in her will.[73] With four codicils amending the original, it was a complex document. Little wonder that by the time it was wound up the solicitor's bill came to £451 13s 8d, and a couple of the beneficiaries had died waiting.

The final list is instructive. If her mother's side of the family provided the wealth then her father's provided the cousins. He had four married sisters, Sarah Perry, Mary Stephens, Phoebe Deakin and Rachel Morris. Since two of these cousins went on to have many children, Mary gained first cousins once and even twice removed. They all received generous bequests, ranging from £100 to £600. Neighbours and servants were not forgotten along with a variety of religious groups, animal groups, a local school and the infirmary. Mary's two executors, William Warrilow and William Gibbs, set up two auctions for the sale of her remaining property in order to create funds for these bequests. The property to be sold included all the land off Maidenhead Road, which was to become Mayfield Avenue.

Chapter 14

Education

When Mary Newland chose her executors she turned to two well regarded men in town; one of them, Mr William Warrilow, was frequently required to act in this way. However, his life's work concerned education, and it was in his boys' boarding school in Chapel Lane that he both lived and worked. With the passing of various education acts entitlement to, and therefore the provision of, education changed for the better during William's career. Unfortunately change also created acrimonious division in Stratford and was to challenge the very existence of his family-run school.

William began his career, around 1810, in his uncle Austin Warrilow's school. Although at that time Austin was the writing master at the famous King Edward VI's free Grammar School, he was able set up his own school in Chapel Street. He did so towards the end of the 18th century and called it the Guild-Hall Academy. It was mostly boys who attended such schools and state education did not exist. The local grammar school, endowed by the Corporation, in theory could provide free education to some Stratford boys. But at this time its curriculum was seen as limited and Austin's school offered an attractive selection of subjects for those who could afford his fees.

For the poor, education was usually left to charity in the form of Dame schools which offered basic education. One such school, sponsored by Mr Thomas Eden of Weston Subedge, was established in 1773 and situated at 37 Sheep Street.[74] It provided twenty-one five-to-nine-year-old boys and girls with an elementary education at the rate of 2d per week per scholar. Unfortunately in 1838 the trustees were found guilty of 'non-administration' and presumably the school floundered. In 1786 a Mr Hutton left money for the education of '12 female children'.[75] But in 1828 the money was given over to the vicar who invested it in the National School for Boys.

Meanwhile a more reliable source of education had appeared. In 1791, the very effective Sunday Schools movement opened three schools. Their main aim was to ensure that poor boys were instructed in the Christian faith, some reading and writing practice was included. With three teachers appointed as many as seventy boys (recorded in 1818) attended at their teachers' premises in town.

Later, when a broader education was thought necessary, day schools were introduced. Two religious organisations took the lead and around 1823 two schools came into being, one initiated by the British Schools Society and the other by the National Society for Promoting Religious Education usually referred to as the National Society. These schools might have as many as a hundred pupils herded into one class to be taught by one teacher (assisted by several monitors). Well intentioned though these day schools were, the pervading classroom chaos ensured the popularity of small private schools, such as Austin Warrilow's, for the better off.

William Warrilow, the teacher

Austin's eldest son James had declined to be involved in his father's school and his nephew William was invited into the family business. In this way William came to live with his aunt Dinah and his two cousins Catherine and Maria. The school building, also their home, was situated next to the Falcon Inn on Chapel Street (Fig 2 No. 5) and consisted of two houses. Outbuildings were used as a school-room whilst boarders were accommodated in the building's nine bedrooms. Extensive gardens extended into Scholars Lane. The boys mainly came from Birmingham where industry was creating an aspiring middle class who saw education, such as that provided by Austin, as a means of improving social status. Austin would have modelled his school on the elite public-school system and had the aim of getting as many pupils as possible accepted into one them. The rest of the boys, who mainly came from town, were day scholars.

The future of the school seemed secure because the wealth generated by expanding industry in Birmingham was not about to disappear. The school was highly regarded with a national reputation that enabled it to sit well alongside the grammar school. When, in 1811, that school passed a regulation restricting to twenty the number of pupils eligible to be on its register Austin must have allowed himself a sigh of satisfaction.

With the unexpected death of William's uncle Austin in 1815, aged just forty-six, events took a turn that seriously jeopardised the future of both William and the school. Austin had written a will and it clearly laid out that his estate was to go initially to his wife Dinah and, following her death, to his two daughters Catherine and Maria. Unfortunately events were to take a rather disastrous twist, beginning with the early death of Maria in 1819.

That sad event was overtaken, in 1835, by the death of William's remaining cousin Catherine. The death of both daughters before their mother was a situation that Austin had not considered when writing his will. Life had continued unaltered for the twenty years following his death in 1815 because William had taken responsibility for running the school. (The 1831 census has Dinah, his uncle's widow, running a boarding school with nineteen boys and two resident teachers). Everything changed with the death of Catherine. She had married the Rev William Barrett in 1832 and her marriage settlement stipulated that on her death the property was to go to her husband. This clause superseded her father's will. Fortunately Dinah was allowed to remain living in the building until she died in 1843. The Rev Barrett was then free to sell the property for £520 and leave town.

William and his new wife Dorothy and child were not treated so kindly and were required to move. They settled in nearby 1 Chapel Lane where William opened his own Guild Hall School (Fig 2 No. 4). He initially rented the impressive property (situated close to Guild Chapel, the site has since been absorbed by King Edward VI School) but eventually bought it. His success was no doubt due to a reputation gained from the twenty or so years that he had run his late uncle's school on behalf of his aunt Dinah. By this stage he was recognised as a man to be trusted with civic duties. In 1837 he was sworn in as the Borough's auditor and a year later as a councillor.

Charity and religious involvement

During the years that William was running his aunt Dinah's school there was a shift in the provision of education that William would have kept a keen eye on. The poor had been badly served over the years. Benefactors bequeathing money to set up educational foundations for poor boys had seen their money diverted to schools for the rich, i.e. public schools that were no longer for the 'public'. (The very seriously rich had always had tutors and so bypassed the whole business of school). With the industrial revolution well under way it became acknowledged by those in power that a better educated workforce was required. Two Factory Acts, passed in 1833 and 1844, required factory owners to release all eight to thirteen-year-olds for three hours' education a day and for the first time state money was made available (state-aided schools). A few rich factory owners, such as the Yorkshire mill owner Titus Salt, opened up their own schools in order to comply with the new laws and nothing but good resulted.

Stratford already had schools for the poor. The boys' British School (set up under the British and Foreign Schools Society) opened around 1823, was situated on Rother Street and was the creation of a group of non-conformists. It had capacity for two hundred pupils with girls admitted from 1825. The National School for Boys, initially sited in Bull Lane and later Greenhill Street, (sponsored by the National Society for the Education of the Poor) was also opened around 1823 and later created a separate school for girls. They maintained close ties to the Church of England with the vicar and church wardens of Holy Trinity Church as trustees. Such schools were financed by subscriptions from supporters as well as by small payments from parents.

In 1846, possibly in response to the 1844 Act and in anticipation of many more pupils, the National Schools were relocated to the corner of Alcester Road (Fig 2 No. 13). This was on land donated by a local resident, Mr Thomas Mason, and partly on land originally awarded by the 1775 Inclosure Act for a hospital for the poor.[76] The new building housed two separate schools, a girls' and a boys' with a house on either side for the respective headmaster and headmistress. It was a grand affair with architecture both solid and impressive. It provided 300 places for boys, 250 places for girls and in 1870 an extension was added providing 250 additional places for infants.

The 1857 Industrial Schools Act was passed to extend education to the homeless, not just the poor. As early as 1828, Stratford had a School of Industry for Girls in Bull Lane. This was later renamed an 'Industrial School' in 1883 and relocated to 1 & 2 College Street. There, for many years, Miss Eliza Gertrude Masters ran the establishment for fifteen 'destitute girls' aged nine to sixteen. It was delicately described by a local resident Susan Buggins, as being a 'girls orphanage', despite Susan Buggins having a friend there whose father was a soldier serving in India. The school aimed at 'educating the girls to be in service'. It was thought that destitute girls benefited from working in the households of middle-class women and the fact that they were often exploited and paid a pittance was overlooked. A survey of prostitutes conducted in London towards the end of the 19th century found that the highest proportion of the women concerned had been, or still were, in service.

If all this change concerned William when he set up his own school, his concern would have been short lived because his reputation ensured success. By 1841 his school in Chapel Street had six resident pupils, aged from

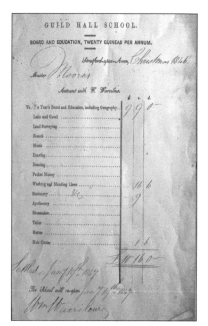

Fig 26. Mr Warrilow's bill for educating Master Moore 1847

six to fourteen and a number of day scholars. His school offered a wide curriculum including the rather prestigious subject of geography (Fig 26). At this time middle-class boys were routinely sent away to such small, privately run boarding schools and, since there was scant competition in Stratford, the future looked good.

The 1851 census shows that the intervening ten years had indeed been good for William. He was able to employ an apprentice schoolmaster, John Reeve, and the number of resident pupils had risen to fifteen. A further ten years on and the apprentice schoolmaster had been replaced by William's daughters Maria and Caroline, who by then were governesses. Worryingly the number of resident pupils had reduced to nine. William's eldest son, meanwhile, had decided not to remain in the family business but had found work as a miller at nearby Lucy's Mill. A decision he was not to regret.

Fig 27. Trinity College c.1872

A new school, Trinity College, set on the corner of Church Street (Fig 2 No. 2), and what is now Chestnut Walk but was then Bree Street, presented an imposing sight in 1872; it also presented Mr Warrilow with a challenge (Fig 27). The building had been bought from Mr John Branson-Freer who had occupied it as his family home. The vicar, the Reverend John Day Collis, paid £1,700 for it and set about creating a boys school which could enhance the prestige of his church choir. It was to be very successful and later became a famous 'crammer' attracting pupils who wanted to get into elite public schools or military academies. It then provided the education that William's uncle, Austin, had provided back in 1810. However by 1872 William's school was back on track and the resident pupil numbers had increased to fourteen. His youngest son, Austin, was teaching alongside his sisters and the school's future appeared secure.

Education Acts 1870, 1876 and 1880

At this time the Elementary Education Act of 1870 had just been passed and this well-intentioned act had created Boards of Education with considerable power. Non-denominational schools could be set up, paid for from taxes, when local provision was deemed inadequate. Subsidies were to be made available to church schools only if they were performing well and inadequate ones could be closed. Ideally, from then on, every child was to attend school from five to thirteen (although children could leave at ten years if they achieved standard six). Unfortunately, the Boards of Education had little power to enforce attendance. The concept of free education was still a long way off and the few pence it cost to send their children to school was often beyond parents' ability to pay. As a result, the Act was largely ineffectual. It had limited impact on William's school over the next decade but the presence of the Rev Collis' very successful college remained the real threat.

William died in June 1873 aged seventy-eight leaving his estate to his wife Dorothy. In a moving obituary in the *Herald*, he was described as 'a man without guile'. Dorothy died in 1877 before she could deal with his estate and when probate was finally granted, in 1884, the estate was valued at just £5. The death of both parents prompted great change in the Warrilow family when Austin, aged just twenty-seven, became the head of the household. He and his two sisters undoubtedly continued to run the school for a while. They were listed in Whites Directory of 1874 as running a 'commercial' school in their Chapel Lane home. At this time there were fifteen other such small schools providing some form of private education in Stratford.

The largely ineffectual, 1870 Education Act was strengthened by the 1876 Education Act. This required School Attendance Officers to chase up negligent parents who were failing in their new legal duty: to ensure that their children were educated. In Stratford Mr Coombes was employed as the first Schools Attendance Officer and paid £10 per annum. The job may have been more arduous than he expected because he resigned after just one month. His successor, Mr Arthur Mills Cox, who was paid double at £20, was more determined and reported that he had served thirty-one Notices of Warning within his first six months. These were notices that preceded court action and were served on parents whose child had repeatedly missed school. The resulting records,describing the destitute families with their 'dirty children', make hard reading.[77] Food on the table had to come before pennies on education and it was poverty, for the most part, that was the problem. There was sympathy for their plight and the School Attendance Committee were 'at a loss how to act' to remedy the situation.

Four years later the 1880 Education Act made education mandatory for all children aged five to ten and the rules on attendance were tightened. The government, for a variety of reasons, was intent on getting more children into education and was prepared to face down opposition. In Stratford, prompted by the 1880 Act, two schools were built in 1883. The Board School was built on Chestnut Walk (Fig 2 No. 1) at a cost of £4,700 to provide education for 125 girls, 125 boys and 150 infants. It is there today and known locally as Broad Street School (Figs. 28 & 29). The other, St Gregory's School, built at a cost of £750, was to provide education for local Roman Catholic children. Situated on the corner of Henley Street and Windsor Street it occupied the site of the old Corporation Workhouse (Fig 2 No. 31),

The 1880 act came about amid much local opposition which had rumbled on for ten years following the 1870 Act. Resistance to the new government Board schools was widespread throughout the country but particularly bitterly fought in Stratford where the battle was heightened by existing religious division. In 1881 the election

Fig 28. Board School girls 1899

Fig 29. Board School boys 1899

of school boards became mandatory. The power struggle that ensued continued down the years and each election presented 'the riotous with new opportunities to throw chairs about'.[78] The religious bodies that had historically provided education for the poor saw the new schools as eroding their influence. In Stratford much was made of the increase to the rates such a school would cause. A poster compared the cost of the anticipated 1,265 children with costs in other parts of the country. Nationwide, Board schools typically cost £10 per child as compared to Stratford's National Schools where each child cost £4 10d. But the 1880 Act, together with powers already given under the 1870 Act, ensured long-delayed changes would happen.

A particularly bitter battle was prompted by the closure of the British School on Rother Street when it's premises were judged to be 'unsuitable'. However, and to make matters worse, due to wrangling, the new Board School had yet to be built and it was temporarily housed in the vacated British School building. When the new Board School building was finally opened on Chestnut Walk in 1883 many parents refused to transfer their children to what they saw as a government school.

The National Schools, on the corner of Alcester Road, managed to survive scrutiny mainly because of the strong support they had from the vicar and church wardens of Holy Trinity Church. Many years later they merged and moved further along the Alcester Road and became known as the 'Willows Church of England School', in reference to the historic piece of land it was built on. It is now known as Holy Trinity Church of England Primary School to emphasise its connection to the famous local church.

Since education was not free, it continued to pose a problem for poor families. The Managers of the National Schools came up with the idea of reward cards for good attendance and punctuality, leading to a prize. Later they awarded attendance medals. These were two-inch diameter bronze discs featuring Jesus preaching to children and adults. The problem continued until education was finally made free in 1891.

The demise of the Warrilows

Something went wrong for the two remaining Warrilows. A mixture of events appears to have precipitated the end. By 1881, eight years after the death of their father, the Warrilows' Chapel Lane School was occupied by a Mr Perry and their sister Maria was dead. Austin and Caroline continued to run their small school, now situated at 1 College Street, with just two boarders. At some point they simply gave up and in 1884 Caroline died. After administering her estate Austin left Stratford to continue life as a school 'tutor' living in lodgings around the country. At the age of fifty-five, he was taken in by St. Joseph's Home for the Aged Poor, in Harborne, Birmingham. This was in effect a huge workhouse where a total of 193 'inmates' were cared for by twenty-seven 'head nurses'. There he died at the age of seventy-five in 1921.

In death the Warrilows were united when they were all buried close together in Stratford churchyard. It maybe that Austin did not share the same enthusiasm and aptitude for teaching as his father but, more than likely, it was the gradual provision of increasingly improved state education that sapped the energy from a hitherto successful family business.

Chapter 15

The 1866 Auction

After Mary Newland died, on the 14th February 1866, her two executors swiftly set about selling her remaining properties. In her lifetime Mary had sold much of her estate in order to ensure that her alms houses were on a financial safe-footing. With her death more money could be raised to provide for them. There were also her beneficiaries to consider, all sixty-plus of them. It was fortunate that, by the time she died, she must have been one of the richest women in town.

Mr William Warrilow and Mr William Gibbs were involved with setting up two auctions for the sale of her remaining estate. Mr Warrilow was the well-respected owner of a school in Chapel Lane and Mr Gibbs was a local farmer. Together they had her will executed in the District Registry of Birmingham on the 13th March. On April 18th, just over a month later and just two months after her death, the first auction was held at the Red Horse Hotel on Bridge Street (now Marks & Spencer). This was two doors down from Mary's home which was the subject of this first auction. Her house was an attractive proposition with stabling, a coach house and two cottages to the rear, all facing Guild Pitts (now Guild Street).

The second auction, held two months later, concerned Mary's Mayfield Avenue land. The auction started at 6 pm on the 13th June and was again held in the Red Horse Hotel. The property was divided into Lots corresponding to those of the 1809 auction, held when John Keen's troubled relatives finally managed to sell their inheritance. The area, covered by Lots 11, 13 and 14, had over the years been owned by Mr Manton, Mr Fetherston and had come together under Mary Newland's ownership. Now it was up for sale once more.

The plan for the auction showed four Lots instead of the original three (Fig 30). The original Lot 14 had been divided so that the house and garden could be sold separately from the land. Mayfield Avenue would later appear down the centre of Lot 3 and the road already in place and running past Lots 1 and 3 was to become Maidenhead Road. For this auction, as for the previous one held in 1809, an advert went up round town and 'particulars' were made available to those with an interest.[79]

- Lot 1, 'Elm Cottage' (now called 'Regency Cottage') with its 'garden, well stocked with fruit trees'. This was an attractive investment with four bedrooms, brew-house and out-offices. It could command an annual rental income of nearly £20.
- Lot 2 was the adjacent two acres divided into fifteen 'allotment gardens'.
- Lot 3 formerly Lot 13, (the Mayfield Avenue land) was said to be an 'excellent building site'.
- Lot 4 previously Lot 11, was 'turf land'.

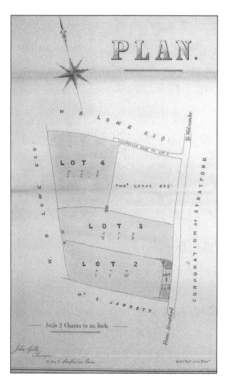

The area was suitable 'for investment or occupation, commanding beautiful views, with good Building Sites'. Importantly it was 'within ten minutes walk of the Great Western Railway Station'. In the 1809 auction the selling point had been its proximity to the Birmingham to Oxford Turnpike Road and the quality of the land and the clay under it. Life had changed over the intervening years and Stratford was now an expanding commercial town with farm land giving way in value to potential building sites for the town's growing middle classes.

Fig 30. Plan for the auction held at the Red Horse Hotel 1866

Two men stepped forward and bought it all. One was Mr William Durant and the other Mr Michael Edwards. The younger man, Edwards, was also acting as Durant's 'agent' when he paid the deposit of £167 on the day of the auction, approximately 10% of the total cost of all four Lots. This was standard practice and was the usual requirement following successful bids. Durant successfully bid for the Mayfield Avenue land (Lot 3) and paid £519 15s 0d. Edwards successfully bid for Lots 1 and 2 and paid a total of £1,707 9s 0d. He also bought Lot 4 for £439 15s 0d. To complete the deal both men had to seek backers for their venture. Durant turned to relatively wealthy men in trade. He borrowed from Mr Daniel Winter, a blacksmith, and Mr John Talbot, a butcher. Edwards turned to more prestigious men in the community, Mr R R Fletcher, a bank manager, and Reverend Henry Leftwich Freer. Both men borrowed heavily to secure the land and both shared the same notion that this was a venture set to make them rich.

Chapter 16

The Sick and the Mad

When the Newland family were dying with alarming rapidity (*see* Chapter 13) they would undoubtedly have turned to a physician to ward off what seemed inevitable. They were a rich family and the cost would not have prevented them from sending a servant to summon help. Medical attention came at a cost and the poor suffered badly. This was reflected nationally until the Government stepped in to sort out quite a troubled scene. But in getting to that point things had not been entirely hopeless for the poor of Stratford. Along the way there had been generous individuals who gave either their money or their skills to alleviate the suffering.

Medical treatment had to be paid for one way or another. If money was limited you could regularly pay into a benevolent society when you were fit, thereby ensuring treatment when sick. The 'Provident Medical Institution and Lying in Charity' located on Guild Street was typical. The charity's stated resolve was to see that 'The labouring classes ensure themselves medical and surgical attendance and medicine during sickness by means of small quarterly payments'.[80] Typically a couple would pay two shillings and this would be increased by three pence to cover each additional child. People paid what they could afford, but for the truly poor with no spare pennies there was only charity or simple self-medication.

The Public Dispensary

At a public meeting in Stratford, held on the 25th August 1823, the plight of the poor regarding access to health-care was addressed. It was decided that a Public Dispensary should be established for:

'The supplying the sick poor with medical and surgical advice and remedies and more especially to afford them relief in cases where delay (too common among them either from apprehension of expense, or unwillingness to apply for Parochial aid) might be very injurious, if not fatal'.[81]

114

It came into being under the careful direction of Dr John Connolly. From the start four groups were excluded. They were the infectious, the incurable, women over six months pregnant and anybody of 'bad character'. Situated in The Old Bank House at 21 Chapel Street, the dispensary provided the free services of Doctors Pritchard, Connolly, Mills and Price. Funding came via donations and subscriptions from the wealthy.

Fig 31. The dispensary building c.1910

In 1824, soon after opening, the poor were *directed* to attend for small-pox vaccination but, this being a relatively new and unreliable procedure, it was generally resisted. The government had felt inclined to *insist*, as was the case in some European countries, but fell short of insisting by *directing* instead. When larger premises were needed the dispensary moved to Chapel Lane (Fig 31) by the site of the gas works (Fig 2 No. 3). When, in 1937, the gas works moved to the Birmingham Road site it was able to expand.

A hierarchy within the management of the dispensary established itself from the start. When Lord Willoughby de Broke became the first patron he was conforming to the rules and regulations that were to remain unaltered over the years, which required the patron to come from 'the nobility and gentry'.[82] This set the tone and wealthy locals willingly came forward and paid their guinea. This allowed them to belong to the 'Court of Governors' and so be associated with a prestigious new venture. More importantly for the poor, by paying annual subscriptions the rich could now sponsor the poor sick of their choice by providing them with Letters of Admission. With one of these to hand the patient would be admitted either on a Tuesday or Friday at twelve o'clock. Out-patient treatment was similarly administered.

The medical officer concerned with the daily running of the dispensary had problems almost immediately. Who, for example, was poor enough to warrant a sponsor? Was a pauper? Was a domestic servant? If financial eligibility was debateable, then the rules regarding illness were more cut and dry. The medical officer was given the following guidance:

- 'Straight forward illness', admittance always with a Letter of Admission
- 'Violent and sudden attack of illness', a Letter must follow at the earliest opportunity.
- 'Severe accident and emergency,' the Letter of Admission was not necessary but admittance was at the medical officer's discretion.

When discharged, the patient was given a Letter of Thanks, which had to be sent immediately to their sponsor. Failure to comply would bar future treatment. God also had to be thanked on the first Sunday possible, at a church of the patient's choosing.

Support for the dispensary became woven into the social life of the rich. Annual balls were organised to raise funds and it did your status no harm to buy a ticket and get out your dancing pumps (Fig 32).

The Infirmary

In 1840 the dispensary became the infirmary offering more beds and nursing care. Doctors, Pritchard, Mills, Price and Thompson, who gave their services freely, often dealt with the most appalling accidents and they, along with the Matron Mrs Margaret Edkins, were required to attend the Coroner's Court to give evidence when an unexpected death occurred. Mrs Edkins had to attend such a court in 1847 after a sixteen-year-old boy was crushed by his father's runaway coal cart. Crushing by carts, boats, frightened horses and threshing machines were frequent causes of death, as was drowning in the canal. Such occasions, one would hope, when a Letter of Admission was not thought necessary.

Access to treatment continued to be via a sponsor, now called a 'Subscriber', and by 1865 the Letter of Admission had become an In-Patient's Ticket. Patients had to arrive 'in decent clothing' with their own linen and towels as well with their own phials for medicine and boxes for pills. Visitors were allowed on a Monday and Friday between the hours of two and six. Meanwhile, the matron had her duties listed in some detail. Among other things, she was to treat the patients 'with good nature and civility'.

Possibly because of the very good work the infirmary was doing it was, more often than not, beset with financial problems. In 1855 bankruptcy loomed. Miss Mary Newland (*see* Chapter 13) came to the rescue by donating £500, a gift that was published in the infirmary's annual report, which also informed readers that 12,961 patients had been seen since it opened in 1823. [83]

Fig 32. A ticket to the ball 1823

The Governor's meetings were usually concerned with mundane matters of finance and repairs but sometimes they were called upon to consider more colourful matters. At a meeting held in 1859, the very long-serving Mrs Edkins found herself in trouble. She had been 'entertaining' her husband in the evenings and that was not allowed. At another meeting after reports of an 'intoxicated' nurse, the nurse in question was duly called before the Governors. Her explanation was that she had simply inhaled chloroform and so was not intoxicated at all. She was advised 'to be very careful for the future'.

Periodically the Governors had the more arduous task of finding replacement matrons and nurses. All seemed well when they hired a nurse, Miss Jane Wareing, in February of 1875. However she was not prepared for what she found.[84] She wanted her own bedroom and to have 'tea and sugar' provided, in line with the treatment of Mrs Coleman, the then matron. She wanted a charwoman to scrub the very dirty ward floors. All requests were granted by the Governors. Later in that month Jane reported that the patients were getting bad treatment, 'their meat is not cooked' and was therefore inedible. Their tea was the tea first used by matron and the servants 'and so not tea at all'. Old left-over meals were 'boiled up' and re-served. Reporting this, she felt, was her duty. Nurses at this time had benefited from the prestige and training that such pioneers as Florence Nightingale and Mary Secole had bestowed on the profession. Nurses now observed appropriate standards which were clearly absent in Stratford's infirmary.

A week later there was a major incident involving both Jane and Mrs Coleman with accusations of foul language and stolen items. The outcome, following the testimony of a third nurse, was that Mrs Coleman was sacked. Jane, the newly arrived nurse, must have felt vindicated and hopefully the patients received better food.

Mrs Coleman had to be replaced so Dr Price was dispatched to Birmingham where he had been told a suitable replacement, a Mrs Mary Arden, was to be found. She arrived on the 17th March at two pm but was drunk and continued to be so all through the following day when she was discharged. Miss Lydia Ware, her replacement, proved to be the perfect angel until 1878 when it was reported in the *Herald* that she had to leave because she was about to marry and the 'marriage bar' prevailed.

A more pleasant task for the Governors was inspecting the wards to see that all was clean and tidy and that the patients were content.

In an undated poem, written by a patient around 1880, gentle fun was made of a forgetful nurse and a cheery doctor, but unreserved praise was given to nurses who plumped up pillows and placed 'soft hands' on fevered brows. To relieve boredom there was quite a lot of hymn singing. A record of patient treatment was kept in a simple ruled ledger where, importantly, the outcome was briefly noted.[85] It might be 'relieved' or 'died' or 'incurable' or 'incapable' (often through 'hysteria') or more happily 'FFC'. This stood for 'freed from complaint'. Severe illnesses involving lengthy spells of hospitalisation also merited no more than a single word. In this way the paperwork was kept to a minimum.

Because the finances were always finely balanced, any non-payment of subscriptions or expenses was chased up energetically. Court action was taken against engineers Messrs Ball and Horton in April 1880. They had sponsored Mr George Gibbs, their servant, for treatment. Gibbs had been a patient for a total of 158 days at a cost of £11 17s 0d. Included in this was a figure for 'lodging and maintenance' for which both denied liability. After the three guineas that Ball and Horton had subscribed were deducted, the debt was £8 14s 0d. The court ruled against the infirmary's claim and made them pay £2 11s 0d court costs. The infirmary Committee of Management, responsible for the court action, consisted of sixteen men of huge power and influence and Messrs Horton and Ball were brave men to take on such a group.

If finances were irksome, much more problematic was the paper trail to prove ownership of the infirmary land. In 1882 moves were afoot to have a prestigious hospital built elsewhere and in order to raise the money the existing site had to be sold. Over the years the site had expanded as more land had been bought in the names of the original instigators. However, Drs Thompson, Price, Hobbes, Morris and Kingsley were unaware that the legal process had not been completed correctly by the vendor, the Gaslight and Coke Company, and by 1882 only Dr Henry Kingsley was still alive. Steps were taken to ensure the ownership could stand legal scrutiny by adding more names to that of Dr Kingsley.[86] When, in 1884, the auction was about to take place, the governors sought counsel's advice. Despite concluding that ownership was questionable, the auction went ahead on the 6th August. The solicitor representing the purchaser, a Mr James Dixon Taylor, needed to be assured that his client would get 'good title' when handing over his £800. Somehow, Mr Taylor was convinced that everything was in order and all was set for a seamless transition from infirmary to hospital.

The Nursing Home and Sick Childrens' Hospital

It should be noted that there was another very successful hospital in Stratford. It was first mooted in 1871 when the Church Workers Association suggested that they employ a 'parochial nurse' to visit the sick poor in their homes when, although the infirmary was functioning well and there was no shortage of nurses for those who could pay, the poor were still badly served. The new service was described as complimentary to the infirmary and no doctors were to be involved. This diplomatic approach was necessary as the doctors were sensitive about any encroachment into their area of expertise. A year later a nurse was set up at 23 West Street but it very soon became apparent that one nurse could not cope with the demand. A move to 5 Tyler Street and larger premises, in 1872, enabled the service to expand. By then it was called the 'Nursing Institute and Convalescent Home'and was to provide:

> 'a home for convalescing women and sick children where they
> may receive medical attendance, good nursing and a liberal diet
> and to undertake gratuitously the superintending and partial
> nursing of the sick poor in Stratford-upon-Avon *without regard
> to religious persuasion*' (their Italics). [87]

As with the infirmary, the incurable and anybody of 'bad character' were barred and admittance was by way of a Letter of Recommendation. The money also came from sponsors. Miss Emily Minet, who was in charge for very many years, trained and then instructed her nurses on how to visit the sick poor in their homes. The institution became a sound training establishment and, in this way, steered clear of any accusation of stealing trained nurses from the infirmary. When visiting, her nurses were to teach the poor, 'how to help themselves by the adoption of simple rules of ventilation, quietness and order and to make the most of themselves'. By the end of the first year 2,727 such visits had taken place and twenty-nine convalescing women and thirty-six children had been nursed under the new institute's roof. The focus on sick children and convalescing women had presumably evolved from the dire need witnessed by the original visiting nurse.

The organisation continued to meet an ever-increasing demand and in 1876 it moved once again and was to be found at 14 and 15 Rother Street (Fig 2 No. 11) in a very impressive converted mansion (Fig 33 to left of the clock tower).

Fig 33. Nursing Home and Sick Children's Hospital 1920

The move was made possible by a generous donation of £4,000 from William, Sarah and Margaret Gibbins. It was now called Stratford-upon-Avon Nursing Home and Sick Children's Hospital. The contributions of those who could afford to pay for the services of qualified nurses provided important additional income in addition to voluntary donations. The visiting nurses charged 15s per week or 3s 6d per day, not at all cheap given that at the time a labourer's wage would have been in the region of 12s 6d per week. The hospital became proud of its training capacity and in 1872 was in serious conflict with the doctors involved with the infirmary when they offered training to its nurses. The doctors took vociferous umbrage because it was perceived as a criticism and a slight to their reputation. They were of the opinion that their gentle guidance of their nurses was all the training required.

The Stratford Hospital

A seamless transition from infirmary to hospital was not to be. The rather fraught sale of the site of the old infirmary was matched by the troubled purchase of land for the new hospital. Around 1882 the young brother and sister, Mr William and Miss Margaret Gibbins (the same family who had funded the Nursing Home and Sick Children's Hospital) supplied £1,900 to buy the six acres for the hospital and they had the obliging Dr Kingsley to intervene on their behalf. The site chosen was on the corner of Alcester Road with Arden Street (Fig 2 No. 14). The trouble, once again, concerned proof of ownership. Ownership could be traced back to 1775 and the Act of Inclosure when it was made over to the church for a hospital, so there should not have been a problem. Unfortunately there was no surviving map. Legal advice was sought but offered little clarity and it remained so even as the grand ceremonial opening proceeded on the 27th June 1884.[88]

Fig 34. Stratford-upon-Avon Hospital c.1884

The new hospital was an impressive building (Fig 34), topped by a clock tower (replicated in the present hotel). A central administrative block was bordered by east and west wings that separately housed thirty men and women patients. Beautiful stained-glass doors and windows quoted religious texts echoing the Quaker beliefs of the Gibbins family, which finally gave in the region of £8,000. Later a modern operating theatre was installed under the close supervision of the devoted Dr Kingsley.

Much remained the same. The Governors continued to exclude the infectious, incurables, pregnant women over six months and anybody of 'bad character'. Paupers could now receive emergency treatment as long as the Guardians of the Union Workhouse paid daily maintenance. From 1894 the infectious were finally offered reliable nursing with the establishment of the Infectious Diseases Hospital situated just off the Birmingham Road (Fig 2 No. 40). This was also a well-appointed building, complete with verandas and a porter's lodge. There were five separate blocks, each with an empty forty-yard surrounding zone and patients suffering from diphtheria, typhoid and scarlet fever were safely isolated and cared for. A separate hospital on the Alcester Road was built for small-pox and cholera patients in 1897.

From 1895 to 1917, patient records show not only the illnesses but also the patient's occupation and the sponsor.[89] Certain problems recurred regularly. Cases of appendicitis and peritonitis were a frequent cause of death in the young along with horrible scalds and burns. Heart complications were frequent and were recorded as 'cardiac'. There were many broken bones, whilst the incidence of rickets and tuberculosis speaks of poverty and poor living conditions. Many children were 'relieved', or 'cured', of chorea, a disease of the nervous system. From 1907, adenoids and tonsils were removed at an increasing rate until eventually the operation was recorded simply as 'T&A'. At that time and for many years after, there surely could not have been a child in Stratford with tonsils intact. Cancer was never a diagnosis, but there is frequent reference to tumours, scirrhus or adenoma, and more generally pitheliomas. Pyrexia was sometimes a diagnosis when probably the cause of the infection was unknown. At that time, abscesses and ulcers could be life threatening as was phthisis (wasting disease).

There were critics. Winnie Morgan, was less than complimentary about the hospital. She had been successfully treated but her poem concludes that we are 'all in the power of these three men, the doctors Box, Hewer and Wells', who 'thinks he's a swell'. Another line 'as long as we stump up and pay the bill' is clear enough although the meaning of the final line: 'and that's how the doctors do you down' is less so, but it's not praise. The poem may perhaps be less about poor treatment and more indicative of a change in the way patients were prepared to be addressed and considered.

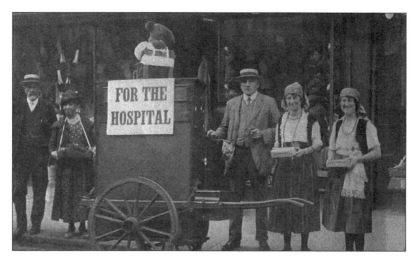

Fig 35. Miss Earp (to the left) c.1914

The funding of the new hospital remained problematic. To help, individuals would donate bread, eggs and spare cooked food. Miss M E Earp, who lived in 4 Mayfield Avenue, was recorded in the *Herald* as doing so several times, particularly during the war. She also publicly raised money, as can be seen in the 1914 photograph Fig 35. For Miss Earp this was part of supporting your community, especially the sick poor who were particularly vulnerable (*see* Appendix 1 for details of her troubled life story). Because sponsors were not always available, it remained the case that the sick often turned to self-help. There was no shortage of quacks and charlatans offering remedies via adverts in the *Herald*. The new electric-shock treatment was seen as beneficial for all manner of serious and not-so-serious diseases. For example, you could treat yourself at home with the 'Electropathetic Belt' if you were feeling 'weak and languid'.

During the First World War 3,245 service men were brought up from London by train and treated at the hospital. Entries in the record book show many limb amputations and toes lost to 'trench foot'.[90] There were repeated 'scrapings' and the 'removal of shrapnel'. Scraping (wound incision) was a new technique that involved removing necrotic tissue to aid healing. This should have been done at the clearing stations behind the front line but the sheer volume of wounded made it an impossible task. The treatment of soldiers raised questions of finance because they lacked local sponsors. The *Herald*, in its 1915 February edition, reported that 'all wounded soldiers admitted to the hospital are to be treated free of charge although no allowance for their maintenance has been received from the War Office'. On a lighter note, even in the middle of this horror the T&As continued. The demands of war meant that yet more money had to be raised and there were some imaginative solutions: in 1916 Miss Annie Justins, later to become a local politician, went out 'blacking boots' (Fig 36). Donations of cakes, jam, eggs, six rabbits and beetroot were a real help in the circumstances

Fig 36. Miss Justins 'blacking boots' 1916

The National Health Service Act of 1948 brought the voluntary hospitals, such as the one in Stratford, into public ownership giving a more reliable future. The governors were relieved of their duties and

£50,000 was offered to upgrade the hospital. This coincided with the selling off of the Nursing Home and Children's Hospital for £30,000 to Stratford Corporation. Importantly, for the first time, the principle of health care 'free to everyone at the point of delivery' was established.

Over the years four groups of people had repeatedly been denied treatment. Now incurables were dealt with by being sent home to die or, if consumptive, to a sanitorium. But what of the two remaining groups, those of 'bad character', in other words, the insane and pregnant women.

The insane

An early Vagrants Act, passed in 1713, had encouraged the incarceration of 'the furiously mad' and so introduced the idea of segregation. With the signatures of two magistrates and the cost met by the parish, the insane were put away in madhouses. If you went mad in Stratford the place to go was Warwick County Pauper Lunatic Asylum, known locally as 'Hatton'.

General opinion, in the nineteenth century and earlier, was that asylums were to be avoided at all costs. Stories circulated about Bethlem, the famous London asylum notorious for its inhumanity and brutality, probably accounted for their reputation. Actually, by comparison, Hatton was a dream. It had been founded after the 1845 County Asylum Act that allowed counties to raise money for the provision of asylums thus allowing for the removal of lunatics from prisons and workhouses where their lack of treatment was criticised. There was a growing belief that many could be cured if treated humanely and that was certainly the overriding belief at Stratford's nearest asylum. Despite this more humane approach, the treatment of the insane remained problematic and asylums were still seen as places of last resort. To be placed in the asylum meant that you had either exhausted the resources of family or your behaviour had become violent.

In response to the 1845 legislation, the building of Hatton began in 1846 on land bought from the Earl of Warwick. The asylum opened its doors in 1852. It was a grand Gothic-style building that held 1,600 patients at its busiest. Over the years the asylum finally extended to over 377 acres and with its farm, chapel, bell-tower and coffin maker, closely resembled a village. The famous Dr John Connolly, a Stratford man, was instrumental in formulating new national rules for asylums and was certainly involved with Hatton.

By the end of its first year, Dr William H Parsey, the first medical superintendent, was responsible for 130 residents, all drawn from smaller institutions. He described the first inmates as between 20% and 25% the 'inconvenient, old and decrepit'.[91] From the outset he did not recognise such patients as appropriate for his treatment. Dr Parsey aimed for better things for his patients with treatment that involved kindness and consideration leading to the 're-establishment of self-control'. Under his guidance many patients were discharged as 'recovered'. He was very proud of his recovery rate and, in 1872, reported that it had gone from 32% to 42% over twenty years. He did not want this rate reduced by the presence of 'long-term born idiots' with conditions that could not be cured and who were, he thought, 'not the main business of the County Asylum'. In 1871, a new building was erected solely for this group, who were then conveniently not included in his statistics.[92]

To show signs of insanity when in the workhouse was a quick way to gain admittance to the asylum. Being a woman also helped. With constant pregnancies, large families to care for, and poor medical provision, women were more likely to fall prey to mental illness than men. The asylum records bear this out with many young women admitted as malnourished and suffering depression, puerperal melancholia and mania.

The following three case studies, spanning a period of sixty-five years, illustrate what could happen if you were thought to be mad and incarceration was required. Getting admitted could at times be alarmingly speedy.

In 1842 Mr Thomas Povis, a Stratford man, was committed to a small local asylum. On the 19th May of that year his father John put his mark on a simple sheet of paper which stated that Povis was, 'insane and dangerous to be abroad' and had been so since the 17th, and with that he was taken away. Two magistrates should have been involved as the law required but one was thought sufficient.

Thirty years later, in 1873 when Mr Samuel Phipps found himself in the Stratford lock-up a more formal process, using elegant pre-printed forms, was required. One such form was used to commit him when he became a 'criminal lunatic' following his arrest for arson. Four signatures were needed, two from justices of the peace and two from any combination of two physicians and surgeons, along with a 'fit and acceptable receptacle' to transport him. With the form correctly signed the keeper of the lock-up could hand him over to the asylum. On his arrival at the asylum the assistant medical officer added his signature and that was that. His stay was short and shows that Dr Parsey's treatment was at times brutal. Despite being recorded as physically of average height, fit but 'rather lean' Phipps was dead within eleven months. During that period he was injected with morphine to ensure peaceful nights as well as daily doses of 'Chloral' a sedative. By 15th December he had gone 'very quiet' and by the 21st March he was dead due to congestion of the lungs.[93]

Thirty-four years later Miss Sylvia Florence Rudigmund Eliot was committed to the asylum on the 21st December 1907 after she was found, by Stratford magistrate Mr John Nason, to be a 'person of unsound mind' showing signs of 'mania'. She had been observed at home 'firing up herself of religious exercises to the exclusion of ordinary duties of life'.[94] Once admitted she was defined as a 'high grade imbecile' - but within two months her delusions were cured and the following August she was discharged 'as well as she ever has been or will be'. Unfortunately, this was not the end of things; her mother, Valentine Eliot, was not happy with this outcome. Valentine had inherited considerable wealth from her spinster sister whose will stated that, on her sister's death, the estate was to be shared between her five nieces, Valentine's daughters. Valentine felt herself to be 'an old lady' and had fears that Sylvia, although no longer manic, would nevertheless 'due to religious mania' give away her inheritance 'to a convent'. Accordingly she wrote to her solicitor at Slatters in Stratford to ask about the 'least expensive way 'to control her twenty-six-year-old daughter's property 'so that she cannot deal with it herself'. A letter sent from Dr Alfred Miller (Dr Parsey's replacement), stated that he was willing to sign an affidavit to the effect that Sylvia was unable to manage her affairs and he could 'do it anytime'. He added that he would have to see Sylvia first. This correspondence smacks of potential collusion and control, the stuff of nightmares. Hopefully she put up a good show and was not written out of her inheritance. The asylum was closed eighty-seven years later in 1995 when Care in the Community was introduced.

Pregnant women

Stratford's infirmary and hospital both refused to accommodate women over six months pregnant. Birth was seen as a natural process and, if you were poor and could not afford the services of a male doctor, a local unqualified female midwife would come to your aid. The midwife would be a married or widowed local woman with practical experience although this had not always been the case.

In the 16th century midwives had been well educated and respected and their skills were passed down through apprenticeships. In Stratford, of the thirteen midwives recorded from 1668 to 1735, three were men.[95] All three men could also practice surgery along with two of the women, Elizabeth Nesbitt and Ann Veale. This reflects the blurring of the two professions and sexes. The fall in prestige of the mainly female midwife, was hastened when in the mid-1700s, the Church stopped licensing them. The licences had given midwives responsibility for baptising sickly babies and this had given them considerable status. Gradually male surgeons took the profitable work away and left female midwives with little income. The training fell away and, eventually, so did the reputation of the profession. Stratford managed with two midwives during the 1790s. They were Mrs Harris and Mrs Niblett who both charged five shillings for their service. Cheaper than a doctor.

Whether you were rich or poor the whole business of childbirth remained dangerous and it was the single most common cause of death for women. Doctors, delivering for the rich, were sharply divided into two groups, the interventionists and the non-interventionists. Forceps had been available since 1635 but little used. The death, in 1817, of Princess Charlotte and her son, following a very long labour, brought this division to breaking point. The nation was so keen to have a royal heir take the place of her hated father and grand-father (George III and the Prince Regent) that the nation's grief knew no bounds. The incident brought into focus the need for more intervention and subsequently the use of forceps was viewed more favourably. However they remained an instrument for doctors and the status of midwives fell even lower. By 1831 the census shows there were apparently no midwives in Stratford, or at least no woman performing that role felt able to declare it. There were, however, seven surgeons - and all were men.

Mrs Mary Smith, a widow, living in Windsor Street nonetheless was a humble midwife. She was not at all like her London counterparts who, thanks to Dickens, were depicted as disreputable old biddies. She was sufficiently respectable to be called as a witness in a case of indecency and exposure in 1847 perpetrated by Mr Charles Thomas Ward of Clopton House.[96] However, in the 1841 census Mrs Smith did not state her occupation and no midwives were to be found in town. Given the number of babies born in the crowded courts of Stratford this cannot have been true. When Smith went about her business she did it at possibly the lowest point in the history of midwives; some doctors were even demanding their total abolition. Thirty years on and the situation had not improved. The 1871 census showed that there were at least fifteen nurses in Stratford but not a single midwife. It is highly probable that those recorded as 'monthly' nurses were in fact delivering babies. Monthly nurses had been created to attend the mother and child following the birth which had been conducted by a doctor.

Fortunately in 1881 the 'Office of Midwives' was formed and this rehabilitated the profession via training and certification, albeit against continuing opposition from doctors. The effect of this initiative is apparent in the 1911 census when many registered or certificated midwives are recorded in Warwickshire. In Stratford there was Mrs Florence Cook, a thirty-six-year-old widow lodging in Sheep Street and Mrs Harriet Sutton, living in Mulberry Street. They no longer felt the need to be invisible.

Chapter 17

Mr Durant

When Mary Newland's land went under the hammer in 1866 at the Red Horse Hotel, two men had stepped forward with successful bids: Michael Edwards and William Durant. Michael Edwards was the husband of Jane Edwards (the woman who created Mayfield Avenue) and William Durant was her father.

Michael Edwards had been William Durant's son-in-law for seven years and their relationship seems to have been amicable. Together they had acquired a large stretch of land on the north-east side of town which, in the latter half of the nineteenth century, was flagged up as *the* area for prestigious development. Both men were aware that being a mere cordwainer, a maker of leather goods, boots and shoes (Durant), and a grocer (Edwards), albeit shop owners, these occupations did not bring prestige equal to that of being a 'proprietor of houses'. From 1866, both men borrowed money in order to buy more property. Michael mainly bought small properties in the heart of town whilst William looked to the edge of it. Jane Edwards meanwhile quietly got on with having more children whilst building up a flourishing drapery business. She must certainly have agreed that property development was the way to go and eventually became more successful at it than either man could possibly have imagined.

William was born in Stoke Bruerne in Northamptonshire in 1801. He married Jane King around 1834, in Nash, Buckinghamshire and in 1836 they had their first child George. They arrived in Stratford shortly after. They were to have three more children, Jane, John and Thomas. William set up business as a cordwainer and there was strong competition. The 1831 Stratford census shows there were forty-four cordwainers; it was by far the busiest trade closely followed by tailors and breeches-makers.

By late 1838 he was in negotiations with Abraham Newland for the purchase of two adjacent plots on the north-eastern side of

Clopton Street, (now called Birmingham Road) near the junction with Arden Street (Fig 2 No. 38). The plots had previously been sold at auction in 1833 when they were described as 'excellent building land'.[97] He bought them with the help of loans from Abraham and Mary Newland (*see* Chapter 13). William was speculating that this side of town would expand, as indeed it did, and that shops would be needed. William built three, later adding a fourth, just along from Shakespeare Street. They can be seen sandwiched between terraced houses on the 1851 Board of Health map (Fig 37. William's indicated with an arrow, now a modern development). William and his family would live and trade there for many years. Four other shops, forming Birmingham Row, were already on the opposite side of the street.

Fig 37. The Birmingham Road 1851

Having secured his place in Stratford, William spent the next few years building up his trade. Being a land owner he was allowed a vote and was listed as a juror in 1847 and 1849. By 1851 he was employing six men. One of them may have been his future son-in-law, Michael Edwards, who at the time was a shoemaker-journeyman. At this time William's eldest son George, aged fifteen, worked in the family business. Jane and John, aged eleven and eight, were scholars and the last child, Thomas, was four. Sadly their mother Jane died four years later on the 13th May 1855 aged forty-six. Her death certificate recorded *schirrous liver*. A contemporary dictionary defines this (when spelt correctly) as 'an induration of a gland forming an indolent tumour'. Today the word would be 'cancer'.

With Jane's premature death William was left with the four dependents aged eight, twelve, fifteen and nineteen and a business to run. Frequently men and women left alone in this way remarried, usually to either widows or widowers who were in the same predicament. Often, this was not out of love but out of mutual need. William remained a widower for twenty years, only remarrying when he was seventy-four years old. Then he married a widow, seventeen years younger than himself, perhaps for love but possibly for the care she could provide in his declining years. After the death of Jane the following years saw considerable change in William's life. When his sons left school they initially worked in the family business, but it was not all plain sailing. George worked well for a time before starting his own business in Wood Street; John left town for new employment opportunities in Birmingham and was joined there by Thomas. Meanwhile, having supported her father at home for four years, Jane married and went to live close by in one of his shops.

The Henley Street property

If William found the business of being a cordwainer difficult to sustain after each son left the business, his keen interest in owning land and property provided an alternative occupation. On the 25th March 1865 he paid £320 for two houses situated at the northern tip of Henley Street, where it curves round to meet Guild Street (Fig 33). He extended his holding by building two more adjoining houses. To finance this development he took out a loan, in 1866, from James Edkins for £400 and in the same year he also bought the Mayfield Avenue land, taking out a further loan of £250.

Fig 38. William Durant's Henley Street property 1932

Five years later seventy-year-old William was a 'retired shoemaker' and a 'proprietor of houses'. He had retired just at the time when his profession was threatened with the introduction of machinery and the subsequent appearance of large boot and shoe factories. He supplemented his reduced income with rent from two lodgers, Samuel and Elizabeth Coleman, a couple well into their fifties, providing good cheap accommodation in return for their rent, this in addition to Mrs Coleman's cooking. Taking in lodgers was normal and William would not have lost any social standing by doing so.

In 1872, William was determined to press ahead with plans for developing his property portfolio and this involved the Mayfield Avenue land. To raise the cash he sold his four properties on the Birmingham Road. At the time he was living in one of them, his daughter and his son-in-law in two others and a tenant in the fourth. He sold them for £850 to his son-in-law Michael Edwards. Although he was dealing with a relative he nevertheless wanted to hold onto the title deeds of the house he continued to occupy. When this was refused he was not prepared to pay the costs involved in making a copy. The whole affair become contentious, something he would repeat in eight years time in a quarrel with his daughter. Later he rearranged his original £400 loan from James Edkins, increasing it to £600. He was, it seems, financially stretched by his Mayfield area plan.

His houses in town gave him a good rental income but his farm land off Maidenhead Road earned him less. He intended to improve this situation by building houses on it. He submitted plans, in 1873, for Welcombe Cottages to be situated at the very western tip of his plot, and, oddly, a long way from any planned road (Fig 2 No. 51). The four terraced cottages provided traditional two-up and two-down accommodation.

William was not being penny-pinching when he built his small cottages with a shared outside closet toilet, ash pit and washroom. Outside toilets, with an ash pit nearby, provided the first managed sewage system and were a relatively recent development. The ash was a plentiful by-product of open fires and was used to deodorise the contents of the buckets in the toilets. In towns the contaminated ash was collected by night-soil men. In all probability William's remote cottages were not serviced in this way and the contents would have been scattered on the land. Basic accommodation such as this was in very short supply and all four were soon occupied despite their isolated position. Today they are sought-after town cottages with every amenity.

The new 'street'

By now William had met Elizabeth Savage, a respectable widow, living nearby in Windsor Street with her daughter Sarah. They were married on 7th January 1875 with William's son Thomas as a witness. William had submitted plans, in 1874, for a semi-detached house on Maidenhead Road as part of his development plan and it was to number 38, which he called 'Hillside', that William took his new bride (Fig 2 No. 44). The house was a step up from his earlier cottages, with an entrance hall and a passage leading to a scullery. However the WC was still at the end of the garden and a bathroom did not feature.

William Durant was correct in his assumption that the east side of town was going to be worth his investment. A photograph dated

1910 (Fig 39) shows rural Maidenhead Road at the junction with Fordham Avenue with encroaching houses. On the 27th March 1878 he submitted a 'Plan of a new street to be laid out and constructed'. This 'street' was to run down the centre of his plot of land and be roughly where Mayfield Avenue is today. It would link his four cottages, built five years earlier, to Maidenhead Road.

Fig 39. Maidenhead Road 1910

But two years later, in 1880, William abandoned his 'street'. He seems to have tired of the whole idea and decided to sell the land and have the money instead. Perhaps, aged seventy-eight, it was all just a bit too much bother.

The 1880 Auction
He turned to Canning and Winter, the auctioneers. They organised the sale for 3rd November 1880 at the Falcon Inn on Chapel Street.[98] Lot 1 was William's land on Maidenhead Road with '4 newly erected cottages' now called 'Welcombe Cottages'. Although not in the original advert, the semi that William had built, and was living

in, was described as 'two adjoining freehold messuages presently in the occupation of William Durant and the other, Mr Summerton'. Surprisingly the person interested in buying this was his only daughter Jane, now the widowed Mrs Edwards. Whether he made her attend the auction to make her bid is unknown. Whether he tried to get a higher bidder for the property also remains unknown, but was probably the case as it was the law at the time. What is known for sure is that Jane and William immediately entered into protracted and acrimonious negotiations. She was determined to own that particular strip of land because it linked the two plots that she had inherited on the death of her husband. With the purchase of this central strip she would be the owner of a sizeable piece of prime development land. She was not to be deterred.

Some conditions of sale were observed with minimum fuss. Jane offered £1,450 on the day of the auction (later the £50 was crossed out) and paid a deposit of £60. The remainder had to be paid before the 24th December, if not, 5% interest would be charged. Articles of agreement signed on 19th November 1880 allowed conditions one, two, three, and eleven of the conditions of sale to be ignored as Jane was his daughter but since they concerned the bidding process this was hardly a concession.

From then on the deal went from bad to worse. All documents concerned with the sale were riddled with red ink as amendments and counter amendments were allowed or disallowed. William's solicitors introduced the condition that, since his home was included, he wanted to 'be allowed to live here for the term of his natural life' along with his wife. Jane resisted including this in the contract by crossing it out entirely, only to be overruled. Another crossed-out amendment stated that the property was to go 'immediately' to Jane on William's death. Having married a much younger wife he would hardly agree to that. At no point was there any reference to his widow living on in the property. After more wrangling Jane eventually agreed to not charge him rent, to pay his rates and to pay for the 'keeping of the building properly repaired and insured… for at least £150'. He drove a hard bargain, but she was undaunted and matched his demands with focussed determination.

Although the auction had been held in November 1880, father and daughter were still negotiating via their solicitors in January. William unexpectedly, but strategically, decided that now was the time to write his will.[99] A crucial clause in it stated that if his dealing with Jane 'was not contracted in time' i.e. before he died, then all was to go to 'my wife and then my two sons' (the third son was very much alive but out of favour). If Jane knew of this, and she probably did, she would have been shocked and angered by her father's hostile action.

William continued to play a brutal game. When Jane was late with the final payment she was charged interest of £11 13s 5d, along with rent of £4 12s 0d 'lost during negotiations'. By now, there was very little love between the pair. To everyone's relief a conveyance document was drawn up and dated 7th March 1881 at the end of which William Durant acknowledged that he had received the bidding price of £1,400. Jane finally owned the land she had set her sights on.

William died at home on the 1st February 1885, four years later. He was, according to the records, a 'gentleman' aged eighty-four. He was buried in un-consecrated ground close to the entrance gates of the new cemetery, a quarter of a mile out of town on the Evesham Road. This was probably because he was a non-conformist and not because of suicide, another common reason. His death certificate gives the cause of death as *natural decay*. He bequeathed his personal estate of just £19 6s 0d to his wife.

With her permission his houses in Henley Street were to be sold. The two gentlemen charged with the task of setting up the sale and administering the will were Mr George Garlick, music seller, and Mr Frederick Winter, draper. They were to invest all the proceeds in 'public stocks or funds in Government securities' and also possibly further afield in 'any colony or dependency of the UK'. The income was to go to his wife for her lifetime. On her death the money was to be equally divided between his two sons, George and Thomas, two successful businessmen, pointedly excluding Jane and John. Both had incurred William's displeasure, but for different reasons. There had apparently been no reconciliation with Jane in the intervening four years although they lived just four doors away from each other on Maidenhead Road. The will was proved on the 22nd April at Her Majesties High Courts of Justice. William's death certificate states that the person 'in attendance' at the time of death was Jane. One hopes that they were reconciled in the final hour.

Surprisingly, and probably unexpectedly, his much younger wife Elizabeth died just months later. She was buried on the 30th May alongside her husband leaving an estate of £110 12 9d. The two favoured sons, George and Thomas, were left to decide how best to deal with their father's Henley Street property now that Elizabeth was dead. The solicitor, Mr Robert Lunn, advised that selling and investing the proceeds, to conform to their father's will, was not now their best option. He was of the opinion that 'no sensible person, except special reason, would sell house property'. It was agreed that the will could be ignored and the property shared between them. They split the inheritance with no further thought of their excluded brother and sister

There is a troubling postscript to the death of Elizabeth. William died at home as he had wished but Elizabeth's death certificate states that she died of *'pneumonia and exhaustion'* at 8 Narrow Lane. Why was she on the other side of town and not at home? Her death was witnessed by Alice Badger who, living in Great William Street, would have been one of her former neighbours. Death usually occurred at home or in the very new hospital on Arden Street; the less fortunate would have died in the workhouse. Elizabeth did neither of these things but died in someone else's home. During the protracted 1880 negotiations Jane had agreed that her father could live rent free in 'Hillside' 'for the term of his natural life' but any mention of Elizabeth had been notably absent and this is perhaps evidence of ill-feeling between daughter and step-mother. If Jane evicted Elizabeth (there is no record of her doing so), it points to an unforgiving streak in her nature. She would have vigorously observed one of the conditions of sale that her father believed had been disallowed. This is an altogether sad mystery and one that, without more information, does not perhaps reflect well on Jane's character.

Jane had been excluded from her father's will along with brother John whilst the two favoured sons, George and Thomas inherited his property. We have seen that Jane was not deterred by this cruel treatment, if anything it focussed her ambition. But what of her brothers?

George Durant, William's first-born was perhaps his favourite because he did all that William could have asked. He remained in town, was successful with his shoe-making business, was a family man *and* he invested in 'real estate'. By 1857, aged twenty-two, he had his home and shop at 39 Wood Street (Fig 2 No. 18). His sons, William and Thomas worked alongside him until they left the family business for lives elsewhere. Daughters Annie and Georgina remained unmarried and at home running their dressmaking business. George worked until he died on the 16th May 1914 aged seventy-nine. Georgina, the last surviving 'Stratford' Durant, inherited the property and ran it as a sweet shop (Fig 40 to the right of Lennards) until she died aged eighty-two, in 1951.

Fig 40. Georgina's Wood Street sweet shop c.1950

John Durant was the son who let the side down and who was excluded from his father's will (and probably from any communication). The reason seems to be that he was a bit unconventional. By the age of eighteen he was lodging in Birmingham with Jabez Coggins, the brother of Maria Coggins (*see* Chapter 12). John lost no time in embracing his new life in the city and became a die sinker (a skilled metal worker who made or engraved dies for stamping). At some point he had an illegitimate child called Florence and lived for many years with his 'housekeeper', Mary Mallin, not marrying her until 1892. Mary did not remain Mrs Durant for very long however; four years later he married Frances Cooper. John was doing well and life for Frances, John and 'Flo' became easier and he was able to employ workers. He died in 1917 aged seventy-four in the city asylum and was not buried in Stratford with the other Durants.

Thomas Durant followed his older brother John to Birmingham where he too embraced the industrial scene and became a 'press-tool maker'. By the time he married he was a skilled worker in the jewellery business. The city was thriving and he worked in the heart of it. At some point Thomas became an 'engineer' and later a 'diamond mounted jeweller'. He was sufficiently well off to be able to buy out his brother George's interest in the four Henley Street houses. Thomas died in 1918 aged seventy one. Since there were no children to inherit, the four houses were donated to the Mayor, Aldermen and Burgesses of Stratford, the rental income to go to 'the poor and needy'. In 1924 the Corporation paid £1,800 for the properties and, under the 1875 Public Health Act, knocked them down to widen the road. The £1,800 was invested and is today managed by the Municipal Charities.

Chapter 18

Working Class Housing

The Mayfield Avenue area and the rest of New Town Ward to the east was where the aspiring middle class were wanting their 'villas' to be built. This demand had prompted Jane Edwards to borrow money in order to own more land there. If the rented terraces of Old Town, to the west, catered for reasonably paid workers where were the low-paid workers and the truly poor to be found? This silent, apparently apathetic group, had been badly served for many years by complacent elected representatives and their terrible living conditions were a festering problem. In this they mirrored the wider country. The nation's population had risen sharply in the 1840s and housing provision had failed to meet the increased demand. Families had no option but to live in crowded slums.

The Board of Health

The 1848 Public Health Act and the subsequent creation of local Boards of Health were designed to change things for the better, although the desire for change was not entirely altruistic: it was thought that with improved housing the poor would be less sick which, in turn, would mean less call on the workhouses, which would mean savings for the well-off, who were required to fund them. Stratford's elected Board of Health employed a surveyor and medical officer, as the law required, and was instrumental in opening the waterworks, thereby giving water to most homes in the town. Refuse collection was finally organised and sewage waste disposal improved when the last sewer pipe was laid in 1859. However, the Board was out of its depth when it came to dealing with dire overcrowding in the hidden-away slums, for the most part located in the town centre. The task of improving them was described some years later in the *Herald* as 'an uphill task' and the slums were viewed by landlords as 'the biggest nuisance in town'.[100] The members of the Board did not see housing provision as their responsibility.

The local brewery owner, Mr Edward Flower, recognised the shortage of housing when, in 1864, he applied for permission to build cottages in Brewery Street. These were to be 'tied' cottages - the right to occupy being 'tied' to employment in his nearby brewery. The earlier 1861 census shows that his workers were mostly housed in crowded courts and small houses along Shakespeare Street and Great William Street. Since his brewery was expanding the cottages in Brewery Street were a pragmatic solution to housing his increasing workforce. Meanwhile the Board of Health's monthly meetings continued to be published in the *Herald* and were usually dull affairs concerning blocked drains, gullies and malfunctioning water spouts. No mention of a housing shortage or a slum problem.

Lodgings

Stratford suffered from both a housing shortage and a slum problem. Lodging was a way of securing accommodation when a low income could not match the high rent demanded for a house. Such accommodation could be found in the expanding west side of town. With its neat small terraced houses this area was home to middle-income families and the retired. The 1871 census shows that servants were notably absent but lodgers were not. A lodger's weekly rent was usually between 1s 3d and 1s 6d and included the cost of coal and candles with the landlady cooking the communal meals. This arrangement worked more or less to everyone's satisfaction and taking in lodgers was seen as the norm.

Rent was usually a lot cheaper, perhaps only 9d, if the lodger was happy to share the family's bedroom with, typically, just a suspended sheet for privacy, an arrangement that must have been common in the crowded slums, called 'courts,' in Stratford. For the truly desperate, if even this level of rent was unaffordable, people could seek accommodation in the very large, very cheap, and very disreputable lodging-houses that were springing up. Stratford had Mr Thomas Nutt's lodging-house in Ely Street in which lived several single lodgers, mainly hawkers but also a family, all crowded together in unhealthy conditions. This was not as bad as Mr William Plum's lodging-house had been some years earlier. His establishment, also situated in Ely Street, housed a total of twenty-eight people, the going rate for a bed being anything from 3d to 5d per week. It was for the desperately poor, those with no other choice, those haunted by fear of the workhouse on Arden Street.

Concern about poor housing provision was markedly absent from Stratford's Board of Health reports until 5th November 1875, when a case of severe overcrowding in Mr Dossett's 'common lodging-house' prompted a debate about the need for 'cottages for the poor'. The debate was slow in coming since this issue had been rumbling around for some considerable time otherwise such establishments as Mr Dossett's would not have thrived for as long as it did. Mayor John Nason had already sent out a circular dated 27th October 1875 raising his concern regarding the plight of the poor:

'The urgent necessity of providing suitable healthy dwellings, at a moderate rent-charge, for the Poor in Stratford-on-Avon, has long ago forced itself upon me and I have for some time cherished the desire to do something practically to relieve this want'.[101]

Mayor Nason was aware of new legislation covering sanitary conditions of housing in towns. The Public Health Act of 1875, made the Health Boards legally liable. He was also aware that 'our Board of Health is unable to carry out the requirements of existing Acts... let alone new ones' because 'to do so would be simply to turn out families into the streets, without the ghost of a chance of their being able to get other efficient accommodation'. This lack of alternative cheap accommodation had, for years, been why the inspectors had not carried out their duty to close down inadequate housing.

The SLDC

The Mayor felt passionately about the horrendous living conditions of the poor and he stands out as quite an exceptional character. He was also a JP and would have had the unpleasant task of evicting poor families. The encouraging response to his 27th October circular prompted him to call a meeting in the Town Hall on 8th December 1875 at which 'The attendance of Ladies is earnestly requested'. He proposed a rather unusual solution, that the members of the Board consider the formation of 'a Company with limited liability' to sell shares set at a low rate 'to enable the really working classes to become shareholders'. He had probably heard of similar activity in London where it was labelled 'five-percent philanthropy' due to the guaranteed rate of return.

Mayor Nason was not deterred by the initial luke-warm reaction of the Board members and went ahead anyway. His new company, the Stratford-upon-Avon Labourers Dwellings Company Ltd (SLDC) published its prospectus on the 31st December.[102] The prospectus explained the reasons for the housing crisis and offered its solution. Stratford had always housed agricultural labourers but there had been an 'influx' and at least seventy cottages had been pulled down. New housing had 'been at a rental beyond the means of labourers'. The resulting overcrowding was 'not conducive to health, moral and general well-being'. The initiative proposed was not meant to be a charity 'which would demoralize and not improve those for whose benefit it is intended'. The intention was to provide 'a good house, a good tenant and rent fair to both the landlord and tenant and a moderate return to the shareholders'. One thousand shares were to be made available the following month on the 22nd January. The idea caught people's imagination and the shares were snapped up by local gentry, solicitors, wine merchants and boot sellers and many others.

The SLDC shareholders held their first public meeting in the Town Hall on 18th April 1876 and Nason 'had every confidence that the undertaking will prove successful' and profitable for the shareholders as well as being conducive to the 'happiness and comfort of the labouring class of the town'.

Plans were drawn up by Mr T Allen for seventeen cottages in Mansell Street and ten on Arden Street (Fig 2 No. 15 & 16) to be built on garden land leased for seventy-five years from the Corporation

(Fig 41). One hopes that the dwellings were offered to the really poor living in the slum courts but more likely, as happened elsewhere in the country, they were inhabited by the better-off working class in relatively well-paid jobs. Following the success of their initial venture the company decided, in March 1877, to buy for £370 and rebuild fourteen slum cottages on Guild Street, which at the time formed Shakespeare Row. They are no longer there but on the site is Shakespeare Court, run by the Municipal Charities as housing for the elderly (Fig 2 No. 25).

Fig 41. Arden Street cottages c.1985, built 1876

During the 1870s nothing more happened, other than the efforts of Mayor Nason, to ease the housing crisis. It was something that the well-off in Stratford were reluctant or unable to face. The unsavoury lodging-houses remained and over-crowding persisted. A case pursued by the Board of Health's Mr Henry Coombes, (Inspector of Nuisances) sums up the hopelessness. A couple with six children were living in one room in Emms Court and were to be evicted for 'nuisance due to overcrowding'. The husband said 'I can't get another house... I've been trying for months... suppose I can't find another house?' To which the magistrate replied, 'We have nothing to do with that, you must abate the nuisance'.

In 1877 Mr Coombes was again going for eviction and yet again it was for 'nuisance caused by overcrowding'. The action was against a Mr John Maynard then living in Russell Court off Ely Street. The case was adjourned twice before action was taken to evict, in the hope that Mr Maynard would simply move out thereby solving the problem - but, as everyone knew there was nowhere else to go. The family were evicted and ordered to pay costs of £1 2s 6d. Having been evicted the family moved over the road and settled in the yard of the Queen's Head pub. It was cases such as these that had driven Mayor Nason to create his Labourers' Dwelling Company. As the Health Inspector repeatedly stated, 'where else could they go'.

Action such as the above was far from unusual. The owners of the courts distanced themselves by employing agents to act as middle men to collect rent and attend court hearings. Slum dwellings were located in the following streets:

- Gloucester Court off Union Street
- Paddock Place off Bull Street
- Garrick Court and Tasker's Court off Greenhill Street
- Osbourne Court and Pinfold Court off Meer Street
- Summer Row by the canal off Maidenhead Road
- Victoria Terrace and Hathaway Court off Shakespeare Street
- Terrett's Court behind Wood Street
- Nason's Court off Scholars Lane
- Cannon Row and Palmer's Court off Waterside
- Russell Court off Ely Street
- Emms Court and Pimm's Court off Sheep Street

According to a local resident's recollection, things were really rough in Emms Court where the tenants were 'always fighting each other'. Meer Street was no better. One resident, a chimney sweep by trade, living close to Pinfold Court, regularly attacked people with a carving knife.

The 1885 & 1890 Housing Acts

At a Town Council meeting, in 1886, councillors were discussing the recent 1885 Housing of the Working Classes Act, which gave them the power to shut down slum property. One member had the temerity to suggest that the council might actively intervene to improve conditions, which was a rather staggering and progressive idea at the time - despite the fact that they had been given the power to do so twenty years earlier, in 1866, with the passing of the Labouring Classes Dwellings Act. Members suggested that they retire to look more closely at the new Act. The Mayor, Sir Arthur Hodgson, thought all was now in hand and landlords would surely act correctly because, under the new law, they were legally liable for the health of their tenants. Prevailing attitudes were well expressed by the Home Secretary: 'it is not the duty of the Government to provide any class of citizens with any of the necessaries of life… including good habitable dwellings'.

Because of the inertia on the part of local authorities across the country, another Housing of the Working Classes Act, that of 1890, gave the local lovernment boards additional powers. Not only could they shut down unhealthy property but they were encouraged to finance new housing, although this was seen by some as a dangerous move towards socialism. Despite this, as late as 1908 housing conditions in Stratford had not improved and the problems caused by too many poor chasing too few houses persisted. The town's worthies were well aware of it - for each Corporation property, no matter what the condition, there were always at least twenty applicants.

At their April 1908 meeting the newly formed Housing for the Working Classes Committee (HWCC) felt compelled to recommend the adoption of part III of the 1890 Housing for Working Classes Act and at the same meeting the Borough Surveyor, Mr F W Jones was asked to devise a housing scheme for the 'front part of the first field on the Birmingham Road'. Unfortunately when he did so it was reported in the *Herald* that it was apparent that there was 'not much heart seemed to be at the back of it', and the measure failed to be debated with any verve.[103] Although a scheme for 164 houses was devised no action followed and there were two gaps of a year each between meetings of the committee. 'Artisans houses were required and they cannot be obtained through private enterprise' was an idea floated in the *Herald*. This was, the first public hint that the local authority might need to get involved, a spectre that frightened the many who maintained that philanthropy and Christian effort, not the new Socialism, were the answer to the housing problem. Despite opposition, it was eventually suggested at a HWCC meeting that the Borough Surveyor be sent to see how things were being done elsewhere.

The Borough Surveyor, Mr Jones, may well have returned with new ideas but the HWCC decided to debate their original scheme for the Birmingham Road. Between 1800 and 1911, Stratford town had grown from a population of less than 2,500 to one of over 4,000. Since private landlords were disinclined to provide housing for the poor it was at last recognised that something had to be done. In 1911 at a February meeting of the Town Council, members were reported as talking with 'no tangible results'. A recent questionnaire had left no doubt about conditions 'you have the result now do something' was the cry.[104]

A week later the HWCC received another wake-up call. The speech of a visiting member of the new Independent Labour Party from Coventry, Councillor S G Poole, was reported in the local press and caused a considerable stir. His condemnation of conditions in Russell and Emms Courts was damning.[105] He had been told, 'we do not have slums', to which he replied 'you do'. He then revealed that in one court (Russell Court) there were eighty-one people living in nineteen one-up, one-down houses. He argued that leaving it to private landlords was useless and the local authority needed to take over, as the law allowed. His single-handed attack caused a rash of angry letters to the *Herald,* one saying there really was no overcrowding and no slums.[106] Another said that the poor were apathetic and happy with their situation, that they would not welcome change. To which another said that 'one half does not know how the other half live'.

The Birmingham Road Scheme

The public interest generated by Councillor Poole appears to have finally got the HWCC moving and plans for the Birmingham Road scheme were put on display in the public library. By late February they had agreed a plan for the first six cottages. There was debate in the press about the appropriateness of the Birmingham Road due to the industrial smells in the area from the gas works, the brick works, the lime kilns and the brewery but Corporation land was cheap and that made the plan acceptable. People losing their homes along Waterside due to slum clearance could now be housed. It was reported in the press that 'rarely has so much activity been shown in Stratford'. Just over a year later in March 1912 the Borough Surveyor, Mr Jones, proudly reported that tendering was invited for twenty-four houses facing the Birmingham Road and there was to be an additional thirty-six houses adjacent to them in a new road, to be called Park Road.

Then the councillors realised that the loan they had taken to enable the 'self-supporting work' to get started was for a shorter period than they had understood and there was a degree of panic . Even so, and much to their credit, an instruction from the Local Government Board to 'cheapen' the scheme was ignored. Despite their good intentions, and for whatever reason, in June 1913 the HWCC committee agreed to halt completion and it was over a year later, in September 1914, when they began the tendering process for the remaining houses. The Park Road scheme was finally completed in September 1916. A Stratford resident remembered the sixty houses being built and being 'quite modern for their time' and that they had long back gardens in which people could 'grow stuff'.[107] They are all there today, with most now privately owned.

From February 1911 when the go-ahead was given for the first six houses to be built it was five long years (and approximately twenty-one years after the 1890 Housing for the Working Classes Act that gave local authorities the power to act in this way) before the scheme was completed. Stratford politicians were in no hurry to take on more public housing and they ceased publishing the minutes of the HWCC as there was 'nothing of public interest'. In 1916, they called a halt entirely: 'No scheme was in contemplation of works to be carried out after the war'. How wrong they were.

Slum courts

Did the local politicians really believe they had sorted out the slum problem by building sixty houses? When the visiting Independent Labour politician was told back in 1911 'we do not have slums', he already knew better. He had graphically described Russell Court with its dreadful one-up and one-down homes on Ely Street (Fig 2 No. 7). At the time Mr E Smith, the agent for Russell Court, argued via the letters page of the *Herald*, that he was wrong and the tenants were well pleased with the houses and their facilities (which he described in detail) for their 2s 9d rent.[108] He must have been mortified when the following week the local Labour Party fought back exposing his lies. They listed, in the Herald, the court's shortcomings which pointed to true slum housing.

It is somewhat disturbing to learn that Jane Edwards (the woman behind the substantial Mayfield Avenue villas) owned all eighteen. They were properties she had inherited on the death of her husband who had bought them at auction in 1869. It is revealing to see how the auctioneer targeted the sale. Posters around town informed those interested that the eighteen cottages, with gardens, gave a rent of £97 4s 0d and 'due to great demand for cottages in Stratford they are at all times capable of commanding good tenants with increased rentals'. They offered 'an exceptional opportunity for investment at a large rate of interest' and therefore offered 'a safe and highly lucrative investment to capitalists'. The acute shortage of homes in Stratford, so acute that the medical officer for the Board of Health could not bring himself to evict families, was a selling point.

The two-room tenements that Michael Edwards bought in 1869 were called 'back to backs' because each house connected to the one behind as well as to the houses on either side. A third room was either in the roof or cellar. This arrangement was notoriously unhealthy with air circulation seriously inhibited causing damp and insect infestations. The 1871 census gives details of Michael's ninety-four tenants: the bread-winners were, almost without exception, low-paid general and agricultural labourers; there were sixty-four children (approx. two thirds of the total), thirty-six of whom were under ten years of age and attending school; those aged ten and above were in low-paid work and only four girls remained in school. Since survival wages could not support elderly dependents they were often sent to the workhouse unless they could make themselves useful.

From the family names that recur one can see that families remained in their homes for many years, often with relatives living close by, as was the case with the Hewins family. The slums were to remain in occupation until 1930 (some even longer) because the efforts of the HWCC had certainly not solved the housing shortage with their sixty houses on the Birmingham Road. It is difficult to be completely critical of the Edwards as landlords. Theirs was slum housing but even that was attractive when the alternative was the much-feared workhouse on Arden Street.

Jane Edwards passed ownership of Russell Court to her daughter, Katie Sirett in 1912, who continued to receive rental money from the, by then, sixteen units. Living conditions remained cramped and a local resident observed that they were all 'dark inside'. Muriel Pogmore, another local resident, remembered stumbling into the court accidentally as a child and described it as 'a horrid little place'. Inside it 'had horrid little tiny houses'. [109] She had been unaware that such places still existed in Stratford. In 1909 the building of such houses became illegal.

In 1930 Katie made efforts to improve the property. This was at a time when the town councillors were debating, yet again, measures to alleviate the housing shortage. She applied to the Sanitary and

Highway Committee to change the name from Russell Court to Ely Cottages. Not only did she change the name but she also changed their structure by knocking them through, thereby halving the total number.

Fig 42. Ely Cottages 1957.

Katie's alterations had been suggested by the town councillors at a 1929 meeting when they were resisting the notion of launching more council housing. Following that meeting Russell Court was scheduled for demolition and the few other back-to-backs elsewhere in town were to be 'knocked through'. Katie had moved quickly in order to thwart demolition. A photograph taken in 1957 (Fig 42) shows the front of the single row of improved 'cottages' and a happy resident, four years before final demolition.

Stratford's 'homes for heroes'
Back in 1916, when the HWCC agreed that 'No scheme was in contemplation of works to be carried out after the war'; they were remarkably wide of the mark. They had completed the Birmingham Road scheme and thought that was sufficient but in 1918, at the end of the war, Lloyd George made his famous promise of 'homes for heroes'. He was aware of the appalling living conditions of the average returning soldier and how dangerous this might prove politically. The 1919 Housing and Town Planning Act aimed to provide 500,000 affordable houses over a period of just three short years. The Government would provide subsidies to 'areas of high housing need'. Stratford was one of them.

Councillors rapidly organised themselves for the first meeting of the Borough Housing Committee (HC), on 12th August 1919. Fifty council houses were to be sited on twelve acres to the west of town, off the Evesham Road. Borden Place was officially completed on June 27th 1922, just two months within the government's deadline and after an eventful and very troubled history. The HC set about creating a system for allocating the new homes.[110] Miss Edith Dickie (Fig 43), then living in 11 Mayfield Avenue and a member of the committee, would have been instrumental in creating the ten categories of potential residents. The first five categories all gave preference to ex-servicemen, the heroes who had come home.

Fig 43. Miss Dickie 1915

Chapter 19

Mrs Edwards

The introduction to this book states that two people stand out as having 'a particularly powerful interest' in the Mayfield Avenue land. One was John Keen and the other was Jane Edwards. John Keen acquired the land in 1775 and tried to maintain control from beyond the grave; Jane Edwards went to her grave thinking that her unmarried daughter would develop her 'estate'. Both would have been dismayed by the outcomes. We last saw Jane as a young widow acrimoniously acquiring land from her father William Durant. By doing so she completed her ownership of all the land in the Mayfield Avenue area. The group of comfortable 'villas' in Mayfield Avenue, and nearby Maidenhead Road were built because of her. The motivation for some of her actions is unclear, but that she was successful cannot be disputed. In today's terms she was a millionaire.

To interpret the actions of the Victorians is fraught with difficulty. Looking back on those days it is easy see massive contradictions and so conclude that they were both the best and worst of times. We can get a rough idea of how Jane and her father William Durant regarded each other when we read his will. It is not unlikely that they avoided each other whenever possible despite living on the same road. He certainly never saw fit to revise his will to include her. How Jane regarded her three brothers is impossible to determine.

Childhood and family

Jane was born in 1840 when the young queen Victoria had ruled for just three years and Mr Guppy, in the town's post office, was getting to grips with the new sticky stamps (*see* Chapter 8). She began her life on Clopton Street (soon to be renamed Birmingham Road) with her father, mother and older brother George. This location was not within the thriving streets of the town but rather on the developing north-eastern edge. Family life would have involved plenty of hard work but would have been more comfortable and more secure than that of the labourers who lived nearby and came to William's shop to buy their leather goods and get their boots repaired. Life continued in this way for many years with each of Jane's brothers joining the family business for varying lengths of time.

Fig 44. Anne Wheler in her bonnet c.1865

Jane lost her mother when she was fifteen and her father did not remarry for twenty years so it is safe to surmise that Jane was responsible for running the home, providing the food and caring for her younger brothers. Education at the time was not compulsory and when it became so, many years later, the leaving age was just ten. William would have expected his daughter to take on the role of home maker and there would have been no criticism of him for doing so. When she was old enough to earn her keep Jane became a milliner. At that time no woman would consider leaving her front door without wearing a bonnet of some sort. Indeed older women were inclined to wear a lace bonnet or cap indoors. Jane would have worked with buckram, velvet, straw and wire to fashion highly decorated bonnets that were worn to offset the cumbersome crinoline skirts (Fig 44).

Millinery was a secure occupation provided that the milliner had an eye for detail and for the ever changing fashions. Back in 1841 Eliza Kenyon, a milliner, traded for many years from one of the shops on Birmingham Row opposite the Durant's shop. It is probable that Eliza's presence influenced Jane's decision to become a milliner with Jane possibly taking over her customers when Eliza retired. If Jane had continued as a milliner she would eventually have moved from bonnets to the elaborate big hats of the Edwardian age (Fig 45). Instead she became a draper.

Fig 45. Margaret Whateley c.1900

Jane married Michael Edwards on the 25th April 1859, when she was nineteen and he twenty-nine. Although both had lost a parent at an early age Michael had experienced an altogether different childhood. His mother and father, Michael and Sarah, had lived a rough life down by the wharves on Waterside. Michael senior was a cooper and died in 1836 just before his tenth child was born. From then on Sarah's life was harsh and the ten-year-old Michael was set to work. His widowed mother and her remaining children moved to the very unsavoury Ely Street where she was described as 'a pauper' and was probably one of the last to receive 'out-relief'. It is remarkable that this young man, having had such a poor start in life, became so successful. By 1851, aged twenty-one, Michael was a journeyman shoemaker and it seems plausible that it was Jane's father, William, who engineered the meeting of Jane and Michael by employing him when, one by one, his sons abandoned the family business.

Once married to Michael, Jane settled in 31 Birmingham Road, one of her father's four properties, whilst her father continued to live in nearby 34. By 1859 Jane and Michael had a daughter, Jane, and two years later a son, Michael, who sadly died before his second birthday and was buried alongside his paternal grandpa. Five years later Jane had her third child, Nellie and in 1873, when Nellie was three, Katie arrived and she completed the family. They continued to live in 31, Birmingham Road but by 1861 had expanded into number 32. This was partly because Michael had brought his widowed mother Sarah to live with them; although she had managed to stay out of the Union Workhouse, her life on Ely Street had been hard. However, the main reason for occupying two properties was that Michael and Jane were now running two shops. Jane was running her drapery and Michael had become a grocer.

In the 1871 census Michael is recorded as both a draper and grocer so Jane was, it seems, being a housewife. It seems fair enough that Michael called himself a grocer but it is stretching credibility to accept that he was also a draper. They were running a joint venture but Jane was never called a draper until much later when she was a widow and referred to then as a 'retired draper'. Such reluctance to have a wife seen as contributing to the family income was widespread in the middle classes and it filtered down to the working classes. The Stratford 1871 census shows that those women who were in work (almost exclusively spinsters and widows) had little choice with 60% employed in domestic service. When dressmaking and millinery are added the combined figure reaches 80% of all women in work.

But Jane's lack of involvement in the businesses also illustrates that as a married woman, Jane owned nothing, a situation not truly addressed until the 1882 Married Women's Property Act. Jane's position in society is illustrated by a court case that involved Michael, not Jane. In 1863 on the 31st March he was recorded, in the Stratford Corporation Police Charge Book, requesting the arrest of Mary Ann Ball, a traveller and a 'known thief', who was also known as Ann Mitchell. She was aged forty-nine and her home area was thought to be Rugby. She was accused of stealing '1 odd lady's stocking and 2 pairs of scissors' from Michael's shop although this was the shop that Jane ran. The magistrate in charge, Mr Charles Flower, the local brewery owner, had Ann Mitchell detained and not bailed. He must have thought that she would run off if left to her own devices. As the law stood Jane could not pursue the case because the shop was her husband's.

At the time Michael pursued Mary Ann Ball, his household had changed considerably; his elderly mother had died and her place had been taken by Michael's seventeen-year old niece, Sarah Edwards. Strangely, four-year old Nellie had been sent to live with Sarah's parents who lived on Smokey Row, Wolverhampton. Unlike the more successful shop owners in town, Jane did not have resident servants. Sarah, it would seem, may have been brought in to perform some of the services of a servant. It is impossible to know how long this arrangement lasted but, ten years on, both Nellie and Sarah had returned to their homes.

Meanwhile Michael was successfully speculating in property. In the 1866 auction he bid for the Mayfield Avenue land. Two years later, in 1868, he borrowed £500 to buy three 'messuages' in College Lane that were linked to another in Bull Lane, one of them being the Masons' Arms. In 1869, Michael went on to borrow more when he bid for twenty-two tenements in Russell Court (*see* Chapter 18) and a further property close by in Ely Street. These had come to auction, in the Golden Lion Inn, after a protracted family dispute, which was resolved in the High Court of Chancery in London. He may well have got a bargain when he paid £715 for the lot.

The next year, in 1870, he acquired two more houses, both in Henley Street opposite Shakespeare's birth place, and two years later he bought, from his miserly father-in-law, the Birmingham Road run of four shops (31 and 32 being his own home and shops and 34 his father-in-law's whilst 33 was rented out), for £850. In that same year he attended an auction at the Red Horse Hotel and bid £400 for 19 and 20 Wellington Terrace, two fine houses opposite where he lived.

A further two years on and he was investing in property in Gaydon. There he bought six cottages and, in 1875, he bought 25-28 Bull Lane for £405. All this investment necessarily involved a great deal of borrowing; it would seem that Jane and Michael were regarded as a very successful couple (even if legally Jane was invisible).

Around 1873, the Edwards family moved from the edge of town to the bustling centre. They went to live at 26 Bridge Street where Michael, once again, is recorded as running a drapery shop (Fig 2 No. 20). The rented property had a kitchen, a scullery and a separate dining room to the rear of the shop. Two large rooms were situated on the first floor whilst the top floor had space for four bedrooms. It must have made Jane's heart skip a beat when she moved in. The shop there today has been extended over what was a very large rear garden that reached down to Guild Street. The four young daughters must have thought they were in heaven.

Michael continued to run the grocery shop on the Birmingham Road (letting out the shop that Jane had run as a drapery) and Jane ran the very profitable new drapery shop in the centre of town. There was no shortage of such shops. Most sold fabric such as buckram, shalloon, black coffin cloth, velvet, cheese-cloth and fustian, fabrics that were bought by the yard, either for clothing or for home furnishing. The shops specialised, some in small items such as gloves and stockings along with all the trimmings that women needed to complete their very ornate dresses and hats. Such shops were called haberdashers. Jane's first shop on the Birmingham Road shop had a run of '34 drawers beneath an 11foot counter' which indicates the sale of many small items. Jane seems to have traded as both a draper and a haberdasher.

Michael died on the 3rd March 1878 aged just forty-eight. His death certificate stated that he had *disease of the stomach and liver, epilepsy and exhaustion*. It is impossible to know if he knew he was mortally ill and, if so, for how long. Would a seriously ill man continue to acquire property and debt as he did? In 1874 he made a settlement in favour of his brother-in-law, Thomas Durant, which had the wording and intention of a will. The settlement stated that Michael was a 'Provision Dealer and Draper' and it listed his properties. All were to go to his wife upon his death. However the settlement stipulated that should Michael's widow remarry the property would go to Michael's four daughters. Future management of his property was to be conducted jointly by brother-in-law Thomas, and his widow. Michael's mortgagors, and there were very many, were all sent a copy.

The 'retired draper'.

When Michael died Jane found herself a widow at the age of just thirty-eight with four dependent daughters, three shop properties to manage, as well as a lot of mortgaged property scattered round town. Three years after his death Jane is described, in the census of 1881, as a widow and a 'retired draper'. Her children, Jane aged twenty-one, Nellie fourteen, Katie aged eleven and eight-year-old Ann were at home with her. They were living in the premises of the drapery shop in the heart of town on Bridge Street but Jane was not trading; the shop had closed and the building had become a 'private home'. With incredible speed, Jane set about a new career. In March 1879, just one year after Michael's death, she had bought the Bridge Street property from Mr Robert Wincott for £700. She was completing a deal that she and Michael had instigated before his death. This was just the beginning

Jane and her three daughters moved from the former Bridge Street shop and went to live in 'Elm Cottage' on Maidenhead Road. This was the cottage Michael had acquired at the 1866 auction along with the Mayfield Avenue land. She moved in order to allow her newly married daughter Jane and husband, Mr Thomas Olney, to run his tailoring and gentlemen's outfitters from the former Bridge Street shop that she had successfully run as her drapery.

In 1879, Jane's two Birmingham Road shops were made subject to new leases, both being renegotiated by Jane with the consent of her brother Thomas, as per her husband's settlement. Remarkably, just three months after her husband's death and this time on her own initiative and entirely independent of her husband's settlement, she paid £340 for 13 Shakespeare Street. She was the highest bidder at an auction held in the Falcon Hotel and we can perhaps read into this an insight into her thinking: she was experiencing a new control over her life and felt financially safe enough to expand her investments and to give up drapery for good.

It seems that Jane had agreed with her husband when he had seen the potential profit to be made in developing land off Maidenhead Road, on what was fast becoming *the* fashionable side of Stratford. In the past, and throughout Jane's childhood, the west and centre of town sheltered the prestigious houses of the landed rich but with the increasing number of affluent middle-class merchants and industrialists, who for the most part wanted their new villas to be on the east side of town, things had changed. Her father had recognised this in 1878 with plans for his 'street', only to give up on the whole idea a year later.

In 1880 Jane entered into bitter negotiations with her elderly father, William Durant (*see* Chapter 17). These were concluded in 1881 when Jane made him a final payment of £1,400. She now owned *all* the Maidenhead Road land previously owned separately by her husband and father. To achieve this she was forced to sell the recently purchased 13 Shakespeare Street (at a profit of £30) to add to the £850 that she had already negotiated as a loan.

As part of her future plans in 1886 Jane paid £575 for 'Hillcote', (42 Maidenhead Road), situated on the corner of Mayfield Avenue. (Fig 2 No.46) This was a fine house built on a plot of land that her father had sold to Henry Roberts in 1878. The reason for her purchase seems odd but can be seen on the 1889 Ordinance Survey map. This shows that the garden belonging to the house ran along Maidenhead Road. Following her purchase the garden was moved to the rear, creating space for the future Mayfield Avenue. An apparently inconsequential detail in a letter to her solicitor sent in 1907 illustrates her ambitious way of thinking: 'will you kindly send me plans of roads for Mayfield Estate which I believe you have with you'. The use of the word 'estate' has an inflated ring. Her father was happy to call it his 'street'; Jane thought on a grander scale.

By 1892 Jane's daughters Nellie, Katie and Jane were married and only Ann remained at home. It was time to change the settlement created by her husband. Thomas Durant, Jane's brother, wished to be released from his responsibilities as trustee; he and Jane were 'desirous that the sons-in-law, White, Baughan and Olney be appointed' in his stead. The effect of this change became apparent in 1896 when Jane made her will and certain town-centre properties were missing from it - because she had given them over to her daughters, via their husbands as trustees. They promptly sold property in Bull Street, The Mason's Arms in College Lane and 4 and 5 College Lane for £1,200. From then on Jane passed property over to them on several occasions whilst she turned her attention to development free from the constraint of her husband's settlement.

Having acquired 'Hillcote' the way was clear to develop the area. On the 1ˢᵗ March 1892, Jane submitted plans for two houses that would complete her run of property from 'Hillcote' down to where she was living in 'Elm Cottage' (Fig 2 No. 42). These two houses would join her house to that of her father's former house and they became known as 'Eastcote' and 'Broadview', (numbers 32 and 34 Maidenhead Road). The plans show two impressive but very narrow, deep houses, one set slightly higher and behind the other (Fig 2 No. 43). Above the cellars the ground floor had a hallway leading to a parlour, sitting-room, kitchen and scullery. Upstairs were four bedrooms and, notably, a bathroom (but the toilet remained outside). In 1897 plans were approved for 'Inchcliffe', described as having out-offices and a studio in the attic (Fig 2 No. 45). With this house Jane had completed her run of houses on Maidenhead Road.

However, on walking into town from 'Elm Cottage' she would have crossed over the busy canal and past the steam flour-mill to her right. At the junction with Mulberry Street she would have been aware of a well-proportioned double-fronted detached house on the corner. In 1894 she bought it. She employed an architect to divide the house into two, thereby creating 1 and 1a Mulberry Street. She also asked him to design a new house at the bottom of the garden abutting the flour mill, which became 26 Great William Street (Fig 2 No. 36). The plans show how cleverly she created three properties with three rents from one. None had indoor toilets or bathrooms. Although Thomas Crapper's highly efficient flushing toilets were by then in production and the town's sewage system was complete, architects continued to design outside toilets.

In 1896, just when everything was going so well, Jane's finances became troubled. Her troubles were caused by the death of a financial backer and were finally resolved a year later. There were also other deaths that meant her financial backers changed over the years. When she had first acquired the Mayfield land from her father, back in 1881, she had borrowed £850 from a corn merchant, Mr Arthur Rowley. When he died his interest, which had increased to £1,650, went to Mr Robert Mansell who, in 1903, assigned it to an elderly widow, Mrs Ellen Bolton. She lived in Birmingham where she had run various successful ventures. She had a sharp eye for business. By that time Jane had already built the first two houses of her Mayfield 'estate' (numbers 1 and 2) and Mrs Bolton would have caste a critical eye over Jane's future plans. She must have concluded that the development was a sound investment. From now on the future of Jane's Mayfield 'estate' would revolve around their financial relationship.

Chapter 20

Suffragists and Suffragettes

As a married woman Jane Edwards was legally invisible. It was not until she was widowed that she could be responsible for making decisions regarding property. Across the country this lack of rights and the right to vote had become increasingly irksome to most women and to some sympathetic men. The first local report touching on the subject of women's right to vote, was published in the *Herald* as early as 1870.[111] Mr George Boyden, the liberal-minded editor, commented on the 'Bill to Remove the Electoral Disabilities of Women' which was going through parliament and he urged readers to support it by signing a petition going round town. The Bill failed as did many others over the following years, often at the last minute when hopes were riding high.

Here in Stratford, a branch of the Women's Freedom League (WFL) was formed in 1907. Later, in 1910, a group of the more militant suffragettes, the Women's Social and Political Union (WSPU) appeared when patience was wearing thin and a more militant approach was thought necessary. The two main concerns for both groups were women's limited rights regarding property and the right to vote. Both issues were closely interconnected.

For women, the right to own property, often called real estate, was reserved for spinsters or widows. This placed married women in a vulnerable position and their fathers would frequently pass wealth to their daughters via dowries or trusts. New widows were, to a degree, protected by the common law of 'thirds' until they remarried so, unsurprisingly, they often chose to remain single. The situation improved with the Married Women's Property Acts of 1870, 1882, 1884 and 1893 which eventually gave married women the right to own property and to keep their earnings. Traditionalists fought against it all the way, arguing that it would make marriage less attractive to men. Instrumental in getting the 1882 act through parliament was

Dr Richard Pankhurst MP, husband to the famous suffragette leader Emmeline Pankhurst and father to the suffragettes Christabel, Sylvia and Adela.

If the issue of property ownership had been for the most part resolved, suffrage was an entirely different matter. Through the ages most women (and men) had been denied a vote despite Magna Carta establishing equality for *all* people. The specific reasons for women's exclusion, in addition to the more general disenfranchisement of the lower orders, often focussed on women's apparent inability to understand the issues involved. With the failure of the 1831 Reform Bill and the subsequent rioting, the 1832 Great Reform Bill was speedily passed. This increased by 60% the number of men qualified to vote, still pitifully small in terms of numbers, (*see* Chapter 4). But by extending the vote to 'male persons' it excluded all women thereby disenfranchising the few women who had previously qualified via property ownership. This was rectified two months later with the enfranchisement of single (head of household), land-owning women.

By the mid 1850's, middle-class women were venturing into activities outside the home with acts of philanthropy and by organising such things as Sunday schools. These activities allowed them to go about in society with a degree of freedom without attracting criticism. The earlier sugar-boycott meetings demonstrate the type of public and political activity that slowly levered women into more public prominence. The Reform Acts of 1835, 1867 and 1884 further extended suffrage, but only to men (much to the relief of Queen Victoria who was no great friend of her sex in this respect). This continued exclusion caused increasing unrest among women including women in Stratford.

In 1897 the National Union of Women's Suffrage Societies (NUWSS) was set up to unify the various militant women's groups that had sprung up around the country, some having been formed as early as the 1860's. Led by Mrs Millicent Fawcett the NUWSS gently and effectively put politically active suffragist women in the spotlight. With their big hats and sashes of red, white and green they made quite a splash when marching in demonstrations. Banners at that time declared 'Dare to be Free'. But progress was slow until 1903 and the formation of the militant WSPU, led by Mrs Pankhurst. Unlike the NUWSS they considered the use of violence and civil disobedience as valid tools in the fight. They chained themselves to railings, broke a lot of windows, let off a few bombs and hindered communications by setting fire to pillar boxes and telephone poles. Over time their actions became more dramatic and dangerous. Emily Davidson died when she fell under the King's horse at the Epsom races. Such acts were seen by many as counter-productive because they apparently 'proved women were often quite insane'. That was certainly the opinion of Stratford's MP Mr Philip S Foster. They did however get a lot of publicity.

These events did not pass unnoticed in Stratford. The letters page of the *Herald* regularly gave space to these events and feelings ran high. The frequent reporting was probably due to the fact that Mr Boyden, the owner, was sympathetic and his wife Catherine was an active member of Stratford's WFL. Mr Boyden was, in fairness, prepared to give voice to all shades of opinion. In 1906 an anonymous letter published in the *Herald* described, in an offensive manner, the activities of suffragettes whom the author had witnessed in London. It spoke of women showing their petticoats and their probable enjoyment, as spinsters, of being 'embraced by a stalwart man', a policeman. The writer also thought that the men involved got 'a thrill and take pleasure that they are holding a real lady'. This letter was roundly criticised in the letters page the following week. In March 1908 another letter described events in London that year: at a WSPU demonstration the writer had seen the unnecessarily huge police presence and the arrest of Mrs Pankhurst. He had also witnessed the way police did 'the moving on'. It was all done in 'an insolent and disagreeable way'. This was a repeated theme. Many letters outlined how ineffective the police were at stopping rowdy men from disrupting women speakers.

For all their militancy and enthusiasm the WSPU was not united. At their 1907 London annual meeting Mrs Pankhurst called for unquestioning allegiance to her. This was rejected by a group of women who quickly formed the WFL. They set about doing things democratically and under the leadership of the formidable Mrs Charlotte Despard the new group quickly gained credibility. Members were happy to break the law and go to prison but were against any form of violence. They very soon made taxation their target when they declared, in December 1907, 'No Vote-No Tax'. A popular slogan that featured on very many badges.

WFL activity in Stratford

Monday 10th June 1907 was the day that marked the beginning of organised suffrage activity in Stratford. Four women met in Mrs Tessa Cameron-Stuart's small school at 4 Old Town. She and Miss Catherine Maclean would soon open their prestigious Stratford Girl's High School on Rother Street but for the present they were focussed on the women's suffrage movement. Mrs Cameron-Stuart was elected president and plans were made to have Mrs Fawcett, president of the NUWSS, address their first public meeting. The Stratford branch of the WFL was born. (They were affiliated to the NUWSS and usually referred to as such in the *Herald*).

By December the group had written to the *Herald* complaining that Mr Foster, a local politician, was being evasive about his support for the movement. A week later, he replied with profuse apologies, explaining how he had inadvertently put aside their letter to him. He was, he said, generally in favour of single women and rate-paying widows getting the vote - but certainly not married women.

Throughout the following year, the NUWSS group worked hard at increasing its membership. In January 1908, during a meeting in the home of Miss Agnes Smith, they resolved that although they deplored the actions of the London suffragettes they admired the raised awareness that resulted and, at the end of the meeting, six new members signed up. During an April meeting, held 'by invitation' at the Free Library,one particularly ardent member, a Mrs Hastings, returned to the subject of radical action. She announced that the London suffragettes had 'done their dirty work' and had done more for the cause 'in two years' than all the 'quiet work we had done in forty'.[112] Seven new members signed up one being Mrs Doonan who had to resign running the post office seven years earlier when she married, (*see* Chapter 8).

In June, the group put Stratford centre stage when members took part in a London demonstration. Mrs Rathbone carried a black and yellow banner (Shakespeare's colours) with the words 'To Be' in large letters and, in smaller ones, 'Not To Be'. Speakers were regularly invited from London and, at a meeting held that August, one visitor demolished several anti-suffrage arguments, including the odd argument that women 'did not have the time to vote'. 'Half an hour every five years' was not asking a lot, the visitor pointed out. Another argument was that because women did not fight for their country they had not earned the right to vote; as Mary Burman, a formidable local eighty-eight-year-old, pointed out in the letters page of the *Herald* paper, in that case 'a quarter of the men in the country unfit to fight should not have the vote either'.

At their November meeting another invited speaker passionately called on her 'sisters' present to have a thought for their less fortunate 'sisters struggling on a starvation wage' in large cities, which she graphically described. Twelve new recruits signed up as a result. In the audience was Mrs Cossins, who agreed to hold the December meeting in her Mayfield Avenue home where forty women attended. She was active in the WFL along with at least seven other middle-class women living in the immediate area.

Throughout 1908, support gathered momentum at a rate that must have encouraged the four women who had sat down together in Mrs Cameron-Stuart's school just over a year previously. In February 1909 at their first annual meeting, held in the Free Library, membership had risen to well over fifty. The annual subscription was reduced from one shilling to six pence to encourage yet wider membership. Those present were reminded that John Stuart-Mill had presented the first petition for women's suffrage in 1867 but sadly the same old anti-arguments were still being aired.

In April 1909 Gladice Keevil and Laura Ainsworth, of the militant WSPU, visited Stratford and at a meeting they argued for votes for women on equal terms to men. They were keen to know who the local candidates were to be in the forthcoming election and they promised 'to hold lots of meetings in the constituency' - which almost sounded like a threat. The election they had in mind was a by-election caused when the local MP, Captain Kincaid-Smith, abandoned the Liberal party to stand for re-election as an Independent. Possibly because of this, the controversial Mrs Pankhurst visited the town on 20th April. She addressed two meetings scheduled for the Corn Exchange, on the corner of Sheep Street and High Street, one in the afternoon, an all-woman meeting, and another open meeting in the evening. Because everyone could not get into the building for the latter, it was rearranged to Rother Street Market. Mrs Pankhurst represented the militant WSPU and when asked if she and her suffragettes were about to attack the local prospective candidate she witheringly dismissed the idea. He was, she said, 'too insignificant'; she was however extremely pleased that her meetings were better attended than his, which raised a laugh. Her speech was articulate, well informed and persuasive and was reported almost word for word in the faithful *Herald*.[113]

At the end of April, Mrs Marie Stopes, the famous activist, arrived to speak at the Corn Exchange. Her thoughtful articles had greatly influenced the women's movement over the years. She pointed out that women were treated worse than 'criminals, minors, paupers and lunatics who could all eventually gain the vote'. (Lunatics could vote in a periods of lucidity). The meeting was informed that members had visited towns and villages and had 'handed out postcards and badges by the gross'. The year ended with many debates and many more letters to the local press. Generally opinion was moving in favour of women's suffrage.

By 1910, many conciliation bills having failed, WSPU activity in London was getting rough. 'Black Friday' marked a low point with many suffragettes experiencing sexual assault whilst being arrested. Things were none too calm in Stratford either. At the June AGM of the local NUWSS group, the meeting was surprised to hear an impassioned outburst from Miss Edith Ashford, a local artist. She and colleagues 'in the shop' (Fig 46) had been rudely treated by the Mayor and Corporation who had 'very pompously made them tear the bills down'. The shop was their very public presence in town on Wood Street (Fig 2 No. 17). She conceded that they may 'technically have been within their rights... but it would not have happened if they had been men'. In the photo, taken in 1911, there appears to be a portrait of Mrs Despard, their leader, in the window. The small posters to the sides may well be saying 'No Vote, No Census'. The WFL was urging this act of non-cooperation in the year of the census and many local women used the census forms to express their dissatisfaction.

Fig 46. The WFL shop (left) 31 Wood Street c.1911

The WSPU in Stratford

In November 1910, the first meeting of Stratford's WSPU was held in the Royal Restaurant in Bridge Street, Misses Venn and Hazel taking the lead. They complained bitterly that so many politicians, including Lloyd George himself, were positive for women's suffrage when seeking election but their support evaporated once in power.

Misses Venn and Hazel argued that there must be an end to peaceful campaigning and they declared that residents 'may be shocked at what you see in the future' – which they were, but in a good way.

By April 1911 plans were being made by the local WSPU for the grand Midlands Suffrage Procession, organised in support of another Conciliation Bill then going through Parliament. On the 21st July the *Herald* announced the route of the march, which was to be held on the 26th, and listed all the supportive groups. Up front the local and regional NUWSS members and at the rear the WSPU members; in the middle would be the Conservative and Unionist Women's Franchise Association, the Church League for Women's Suffrage, the Men's League for Women's Suffrage and the Men's Political Union for Women's Suffrage. Miss Hazel would speak for the WSPU and Miss Timpany and Mrs Ring would do the same on behalf of the NUWSS.

Fig 47. The Midlands Suffrage Procession 1911

A week later the press reported in great detail on what a grand day out it had been. It described the red, green and white sashes of the NUWSS (green for hope, white for faith, red for love) and the purple, white and green of the WSPU (purple for dignity, white for purity, green for hope). As expected there was a fair number of banners, along with bunting and foliage on the wagons (Fig 47). The town band performed and marched splendidly. The wide-ranging speeches of Lady Willoughby De Broke (founder member of the Conservative and Unionists Women's Franchise Association) and Lady Selbourne were well informed. They certainly knew their facts, what's more they had a letter from the local MP Mr Foster pledging his support for the new Conciliation Bill - which of course he failed to do despite a 'memorial' with 388 signatures of support sent to him from local residents. His about-turn was explained at the 1912 AGM of the local NUWSS - his change of tune had apparently been caused by the militancy of some of the Suffragist groups. This was echoed in a long letter published in the *Herald* from Millicent Fawcett, the NUWSS leader, in which she said their actions had cost a possible thirty-five votes in parliament.[114] All members felt hugely let down.

The NUWSS Pilgrimage

By June 1913 there was excitement in town because a branch of the great NUWSS pilgrimage from Carlisle to London was due to arrive the following month. The editor of the *Herald* was of the opinion that a pilgrimage was a good way to publicise the cause in preference 'to smashing things up and starving in jail'. The women marchers were required to wear white, grey, black and navy clothes. Since they all wore sashes of red, green and white they appeared as a united and attractive group. Some rode bicycles and others rode horses but the majority walked. The eight different routes through towns and villages were to meet for a demonstration in Hyde Park on the 26th July. With women joining and leaving the procession along its route very many were involved. The plan was for the Watling Street route to make a small detour to Stratford on the 16th July. Four days previously Lady Willoughby De Broke, of Compton Verney, held an 'at home' during which she was pleased to report that there were about sixty women marching and that they had all been 'politely received' in the towns along the way. Unfortunately, that changed when the women arrived at Stratford.

Their organisation had been faultless. With the route round town planned and the proposed site in Rother Street set up for the speakers at 8 pm, all was prepared and another grand day out was expected; the Leamington Town Band was assembled and ready to march. To start with, all went to plan; the fifty-six women arrived in town at 4 pm and were politely received and went off to lay a wreath at Shakespeare's grave. They then joined the band and processed round town ready to meet at Rother Street fountain. A crowd had gathered and speakers were named and welcomed (Fig 48 probably of this meeting).

Fig 48. The NUWSS Pilgrimage from Carlisle to London 1913

Then a large crowd of rowdy men began to heckle, boo, jeer and catcall. At this point, women in the crowd were 'roughly treated' but the police stood by and only escorted one man away when he became particularly obnoxious. For a while a suffragist called Miss Margaret Ashton dealt exceedingly well with the hecklers, answering their sarcastic calls effectively and most of her speech, covering wages and housing conditions, was heard and reported before she gave up and Miss Patience Hanbury took over. But by this time things were disintegrating so the organisers tried a 'double move': they arranged for the speakers to be at 'both ends of the platform'.

At one point when Mrs Despard's sister, Mrs Katherine Harley, was speaking, dangerous and 'ugly moves' by some in the crowd caused the police to move to the front to protect her, but at least she was given 'a fair hearing'. But when Miss Hanbury, the other speaker, finally gave up trying to be heard, the mob rushed at Mrs Harley forcing her also to retire and so the meeting was abandoned. This unfortunate turn of events was reported nationally and general opinion held that the rowdy opposition had been organised well in advance and that the police had been ineffective. The local *Herald* had reported all the events and an editorial expressed 'shame and regret at the violence shown by some contemptible rascals' and 'those who championed the cause… were rather hardly dealt with by a section of the crowd'. No arrests were made at the time.

A week later Mr Frank Ryman was brought before Mr Boyden in the Magistrates Court on a triple-assault charge. The offences occurred after the meeting when feelings were still at boiling point. A crowd of over twenty-five men had been harassing Mr Gruenwald and Mr and Mrs Frederick Guyver had offered sanctuary in their nearby Wood Street shop but, due to the excited nature of the growing crowd, the three didn't make it that far and were forced to flee to the back yard of the 'Horse and Jockey'. While trying to climb over the back wall, trousers were torn and both Mr and Mrs Guyver's hats were knocked off. The pair felt obliged to declare that they were not in sympathy with the suffragists in an attempt to pacify the mob; by then, fifty to sixty people were involved. Given Mr Boyden's openly declared sympathy for the suffragist cause, Ryman must have felt himself unlucky to get hauled up before him. He was found guilty of three assaults, fined a total of £2 13s 0d including costs, and had to pay up within a month or spend six weeks in jail. He complained at the severity of this and said, it 'would take all the money I can earn in six weeks' to pay it. Boyden suggested he 'should have thought of this before' and added that perhaps his numerous mates could chip in.

Public meetings continued throughout the remainder of 1913, unaffected by the rumpus of the National Pilgrimage. At one boisterous meeting, held in November, WSPU member Miss Wylie described the severe injuries inflicted on militants in London, especially during force-feeding.

Local anti-suffrage groups usually held their meetings in the Corn Exchange. Women who were against the vote used arguments such as those illustrated in the many private letters written by Rebecca Dulcibella Dering, a rich land owner from nearby Baddsley Clinton.[115] Women were 'not constitutionally fit' to vote, claimed Dering, and they could not debate 'without bias, sentiment or passion'. They might be instructed as to how to vote by their husbands but would 'change their minds at the last moment and vote as they pleased...God almighty never fitted them for such duties'. Similar thoughts were expressed by Miss Marie Corelli, the famoue authoress, who lived on Church Street. In her 'Woman or Suffragette, a Question of Choice' published in 1907 she argued that men should be left to rule because a woman 'has no need to come down from her throne and mingle in any of his political frays'. 'I have no politics and want none', said Marie Corelli and she circulated pamphlets to this effect. She had a change of heart in 1919 when the fight was over.

When war began in 1914 the NUWSS announced, via the pages of the *Herald*, that it was suspending action. This did not stop the occasional letter being published. One, printed in 1917, condemned a resurgence in suffragist activity in London as 'opportunistic' when men were fighting at the front and parliament was 'over worked'. At a meeting of the local National League for Opposing Women's Suffrage a resolution was passed, presented by Lady Fairfax Lucy of Charlecote Park, to be sent to Asquith, deploring suffragist action that 'deflects from the efficient conduct of the war'.

It would seem that it took a war to get things changed. Women having stepped into men's jobs, it was seen as unacceptable to withhold the vote once the war was over. In 1918 David Lloyd George and Emmeline Pankhurst secretly worked together to organise a procession in support of the Representation of the People Bill, which passed by 385 votes to 55. The 8.4 million women who gained the vote did so if they were over thirty and were householders or married to householders, or an occupier of property with an annual rent of £5 or a graduate of a British university or equivalent study. There was also a massive gain for men (approx. 40%) because all were now included if over the age of twenty-one. The age difference was mainly to prevent women outnumbering men at the polling stations since so many men had died during the war.

The Representation of the People Act of 1918 changed the size of the total electorate from 7.7 million to 21.4 million, with women making up 43% of the total. It must be noted however that many of the young women who worked to aid the war effort were still excluded. In 1928 a further act was passed abolishing the property requirement and equalising the eligible age to twenty-one. Women's voting rights were at last brought completely into line with those of men.

Chapter 21

The Mayfield 'Estate'

A t the turn of the century Jane Edwards left Stratford, the town of her birth. She had endured a truly bad few years as her widowed daughter, Jane Olney, gradually slid into debt as she developed her new guest-house business (*see* Appendix 4). The humiliation of the 1906 public meetings, held in the Red Horse Hotel, where creditors called her daughter to account, may well have prompted Jane to move to nearby Leamington Spa. But she had Ann, her unmarried daughter, to consider. Jane understood that there was little chance of her thirty-year-old spinster-daughter marrying and she wanted to secure Ann's future. Property development had served her well as a widow so why should it not also serve Ann? Jane had already begun her Mayfield 'Estate' and so sought to include Ann. Unfortunately, Ann, an accomplished portrait artist, was perhaps not quite as interested as her mother might have wished. From 1903 onwards, the erratic development of Mayfield Avenue was managed by both Jane and Ann in various combinations.

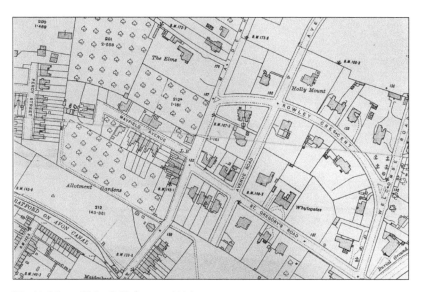

Fig 49. Map of Mayfield Avenue 1914

A section of the 1914 OS map of the area (Fig 49) shows Mayfield Avenue development up to the death of Jane in July 1915. Her seven properties on the adjoining Maidenhead Road can also be seen as well as the four cottages previously built by her father at the western tip of the land. Back in 1903 the land had been just fields; prestigious 'villas' were about to appear.

From the start Jane placed restrictions in the deeds of sale whenever she sold either land or property, thereby ensuring that Mayfield Avenue remained select. She was insistent that the owners did not 'carry on or permit noxious or noisy or offensive trade or business or manufacture whatsoever nor the trade or business of an Innkeeper or dealer in wine ale beer or spirits'. No building was to be erected other than a 'private dwelling house with necessary outbuildings'. She was keen to keep the rateable value of each property high, at not less than £17pa, which ensured that none but substantial 'villas' could be built and that the area would remain residential. At this time the local rates paid for amenities that included inspectors for 'Nuisances and Canal Boats', 'Bathing Places and the River' and 'Fountains and Urinals'.

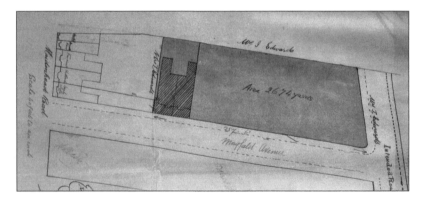

Fig 50. Plan showing Ann's land and her two houses 1903

In 1903 Jane sold a strip of the Mayfield land to Ann for £100 (along with the semi-detached houses she had built earlier in 1902). Ann needed to borrow money for this and turned to her mother's new financier, Mrs Ellen Bolton. In a letter dated November 4th Mrs Bolton wrote that she was happy to lend the money 'at once' and could 'stretch to £150 if required' and would be pleased to get the '4% interest'. Mrs Bolton was clearly of the same opinion as Jane that this was an area ripe for development. Ann's land (Fig 50) was sandwiched between her mother's land and was to become the south side of Mayfield Avenue.

The 'intended road' marked on the map not only linked the four older cottages, built earlier by Jane's father, to her avenue but also kept open the option for further development to the north and south. This subsequently happened to the north (now St Mary's Road), but not until after the Second World War and was not initiated by Ann as her mother would have hoped.

Numbers 1 and 2

Fig 51. Numbers 1 and 2 (called 'Ipsley' in 1908), 2017 courtesy P Loe

A pair of semi-detached houses, (soon to become numbers 1 and 2 Mayfield Avenue), had already been built by Jane and became Ann's when she bought her strip of land(Fig 2 No. 47). The houses were well-appointed 'villa residences' each having a spacious hallway and the new inside toilets although still no bathroom (Fig 51). The tenants,

Mr Hodges and Mrs Sykes, were hopefully well content with the facilities even though at that time the road was still mud. The villas remained in Ann's ownership for many years and gave her the income her mother had planned.

Numbers 3-9

Ann's first move was to obtain planning approval for a terrace of seven 'villa residences' next to her two recently acquired villas. With Mr W Price as her architect, building began in December 1903. In 1904, Ann had to raise a £700 mortgage and she chose to turn to a building society and not to Mrs Bolton, as previously. At first she seems to have been just as able as her mother but something went awry because only numbers 3, 4 and 5 were completed (Fig 2 No. 48). The

Fig 52. Number 5, (called 'Lindridge' in 1931), 2017 courtesy P Loe

fourth villa, number 6, was built quite a while later, when in October 1907, Stephen White, a 'gent' from Court Leigh, Malvern, stepped in with £61 19s 0d and bought the plot. Having built the house he sold it three years later. The remaining three villas, numbers 7, 8 and 9 were abandoned. Number 3 remained in Ann's ownership for many years but she sold numbers 4 and 5 to a Mr Charles Earp who installed his mother and two sisters in number 4 and rented out number 5, the house that inspired this story (Fig 52 *see* Appendix 1 for further details). He extended the gardens in 1920 when he bought 'garden land' from Ann.

Numbers 11 and 12

Fig 53. No. 11, 2017 courtesy P Loe

Whilst Ann was attempting to develop her terrace, Jane was planning the attractive semi-detached house on the opposite side of the road, numbers 11 and 12 (Fig 53 & Fig 2 No. 53). Because of the narrowness of the plot the houses had small back gardens but long side gardens. Mr W Price was once again the architect and plans were approved on the 11th April 1905 and the building was completed well within the year. Jane retained number 11 for renting, calling it 'Orchards' and continued to own it until she died, at which time it was passed to her daughter Katie.

Number 12 was sold to the Chandler sisters in 1905 but, unaccountably, Jane dragged out the whole business, causing everyone concerned considerable fuss and bother. The purchasers were two middle-aged sisters, Miss Harriet Leavers Chandler and Miss Celia Agnes Chandler. They ran a school in Rother Street and intended to run a larger one in this more prestigious part of town. Along with them came their father, the Reverend Charles Chandler, a Congregational Minister. A curt letter from Miss Harriet Chandler, written on the 13th July 1905, shows that they had been in discussions regarding the sale for some time and that they 'want it settled' because they 'expect to go for our holiday'. The letter had been preceded by many others, all expressing concern regarding liability for the cost of the road, which the Chandlers successfully refused to accept. Then, in August 1905, their solicitor demanded proof of Jane's title to the land and only when this last problem was resolved, was the business concluded.

Fig 54. The Chandlers with their pupils c.1906/7

The sisters called their new school 'Belmont' and local women remember attending. One of them, Mary Williams, said from being a healthy child she became ill with all sorts of diseases, measles included, because the forty pupils were 'packed' into the school (Fig 54) which made it an unhealthy place for the children. In 1912 the sisters rented the house to a Miss Annie Hubbard who for twenty-one years used it to run a 'girls finishing school' where elocution lessons were on the curriculum. A pupil of theirs, Mabel Burton, remembered having 'a Belgian man to teach French'. He was possibly a refugee during the First World War (*see* Chapter 22).

Number 10a

Fig 55. Number 10a, 2017 courtesy P Loe

If the Chandler sisters had caused Jane sleepless nights then Mrs Edith Blanche Cossins had much the same affect when, in 1907, she bought the plot of land adjacent to number 11 (Fig 2 No. 52). Mrs Cossins planned to build, what would be number 10a, and she chose Mr J Cox as both her architect and builder (Fig 55). The stylish new bungalow was approved in May 1907 but before this Jane turned the process into a protracted and disagreeable affair, possibly because Mrs Cossins had not followed Jane's standard style of design and had found her own architect and builder. During the previous February, letters sped from Mrs Cossins' Birmingham solicitors to Jane. Initially they concerned the cost of the road and later they focussed on the nature of the proposed fencing. Jane dragged matters out until an irate Mrs Cossins wrote, 'be so good as to hurry up the settlement of the purchase of the land... such a long delay is unnecessary'. At last Jane approved and building began. The house was called 'St Issey' in 1911 and 'The Bungalow' in 1916.

Jane Edwards and her daughter Ann completed seven houses and sold two plots in the burst of development between 1902 and 1907, then they paused. Perhaps both women had become a little disenchanted with the building business. Jane had experienced abrasive encounters with Mrs Cossins and something had stopped Ann from completing her terrace. In addition, Jane was having problems with her financial backer Mrs Bolton.

Mrs Bolton had taken over Jane's mortgage from Mr Robert Mansell in 1903 but soon after began to express concern about the security of her investment. In 1907 she requested details of rental income from all the properties she had an interest in. She was unhappy that Jane was selling off land and houses. In a letter dated 29th April, Mrs Bolton's solicitor indicated that although she worried 'more than the facts justify', she really should not have to worry, whether justified or no, given her age. They might therefore 'consider whether the money should be called in'. This series of letters must have rocked any confidence Jane had in Mrs Bolton's support for her venture and Jane asked her solicitor to find a younger financier. On 1st October 1908, three years later, she was asking for a person who might have a similar sum to invest who not only lived nearer than Mrs Bolton but who might also be agreeable to selling off land.

Mrs Bolton meanwhile knew nothing of Jane's thoughts. In 1910, relations were still sufficiently amicable that when Ann bought 'Hillside', 38 Maidenhead Road (formally her grandfather's home), from her mother for £250, she was helped financially by Mrs Bolton. It was not until March 1912, two years later, that things came to a head. Mrs Bolton sent Jane a letter asking her to return the original stake of £1,650 and in this way their business relationship came to an end.

Number 7

Fig 56. Number 7, called variously,
'The Digley', 'Helston' and 'Lynton', c.1920

Ann decided to sell land without developing it, perhaps because her heart was never in the business. In April 1908 she sold a plot, forty-seven feet long, adjacent to the last property in her terrace. At first all went very well. In an early letter, written in June, she urged her solicitor to act 'with as little delay as possible'. The prospective purchaser, Mr Robert Lunn, a local solicitor, gained planning approval on 16th July and as he planned to make use of Price & Sons as architects a trouble-free venture was expected.

However, Mr Lunn, soon to be elevated to Town Clerk, did not complete the deal until 20th January 1909. The delay was caused by his over-cautious approach which irritated Ann, which she did little to hide. Mr Lunn created 'covenants' governing not only his own land but also the development of the remaining seventy-three-foot plot. He wanted assurances that his prestigious new house (Fig 56) would not be devalued or overlooked by inferior development.

Completion in January followed an earlier letter from an exasperated Ann: that she was tired of 'the unnecessary trouble caused' by him. She felt that she had 'agreed to the other conditions most unwillingly and must decline to agree to any more… he can take it or leave it'. A remarkably confident stand for a young art teacher to take. She was not intimidated by his reputation. Conflict continued over the issue of the cost of the road (in handwriting of a style remarkably similar to that of her mother) which finally ended when Ann's solicitor advised her to give in and accept liability. With aggrieved resignation Mr Lunn completed the deal and the house was finally built (Fig 2 No. 49).

Numbers 8, 9 and 10.

Fig 57. Numbers 8, 9 and 10, courtesy P Loe

While Ann was battling with Mr Lunn in 1909, Jane set about developing the plot for numbers eight, nine and ten (Fig 2 No. 50). They were to be on the other side of her 'intended road' looking down Mayfield Avenue. Once again Price & Sons designed and built the terrace. They were similar in design to the existing terrace but had the additional attraction of fashionable French windows (Fig 57). By 1910 the avenue was complete.

With all the houses in place, Jane was obliged to get on with the road. She had caused friction and delay when she tried to get Mr Lunn, Mrs Cossins and the Chandlers to accept some liability for cost; she did not 'wish to bind myself to make any of the proposed roads'. But she eventually capitulated and work began in November 1909. The road was completed in June 1910 at a cost of £54 10s 8d at which time Jane had fourteen days in which to pay the costs.

At this point it would seem that Jane, like her father before her, decided to retire from property development. But unlike him she wanted to support her daughter to continue what she had begun. She chose to ignore the fact that Ann was possibly jeopardising her whole plan when she sold number 4 Mayfield Avenue in 1908 and was set to sell number 5. Nevertheless in 1911, with the consent of the trustees (her three sons-in-law), Jane gave over to her daughter Ann, 'Elm Cottage' (30 Maidenhead Road) and all the associated land that her husband and father had bought in the 1866 auction (*see* Chapter 17). Anne's holdings were further increased when Jane died four years later in 1915. Jane had ensured that her one unmarried daughter was financially secure and had the means to further develop her 'estate'.

But she didn't. In 1928, thirteen years after having control of the whole Mayfield area Ann put the land and properties up for auction. The paperwork shows that Ann had become Mrs Joseph W Jubb. She had married in 1921 at the grand old age of forty-eight, something her mother could never have imagined. At the time of the auction she was living in 'Elm Cottage' but left town once the sale was completed. Ann was finally free of her mother's 'estate'. The 'estate' was her mother's dream, not hers.

Chapter 22

World War One

If Jane Edwards felt a sense of relief when Mayfield Avenue was completed in 1910 it would have been over-shadowed by anguish when the country went to war. Although most families in Stratford undoubtedly experienced the collective pain of losing a father, brother or son, along with this came a sense of purpose and community. The record of events in the town during the war is, by its very nature, predominately about the women left behind. Many volunteered for activities that would have otherwise been frowned upon. In this the women of Stratford were representative of women across the country who volunteered on a grand scale and experienced a new sense of freedom. When the carnage finally came to an end, the predominantly Victorian way of life which had existed before the war was challenged.

Fig 58. Recruitment day on Bridge Street, 1915

At the start there was the excitement of recruitment days with their powerful brew of patriotism and bravado, designed to encourage young men to step up and sign up. One such day was held on Bridge Street in November, just three months after Britain's declaration of war (Fig 58). The older soldiers look as though they know the score, which they would have, since many of them were sergeants and may have served in the Boer Wars. The soldier with the stick may well be Captain Grant who was responsible for drumming up recruits. He and his staff enlisted 167 men in just two months that autumn and by February 1915 the figure had become 401.

Patriotism and bravado played a part in Captain Grant's successful recruitment drive and these feelings were heightened by the surprise shelling, in January 1915, from German naval vessels, of the east-coast towns of Hartlepool, Whitby and Scarborough. It was generally understood that the war would be a short one but Lord Kitchener, made Secretary of State for War in 1914, thought differently. In January 1915 the *Herald* quoted Kitchener's sister saying that her brother had told her 'the war will last a bit longer, in fact a good deal longer. The longer it lasts, the more men will be required, and more men we must have'. It did last longer, and he did get his men. At least at the start.

Kitchener's severe image on recruitment posters with finger pointing at YOU was said, in some quarters, to have been counter-productive. Certainly the *Herald* held it to be so. The editor claimed that it was 'for each man to make up his own mind'. Although the Parliamentary Recruiting Committee initially refused to use it on official posters, it went on to become one of the most successful recruiting images of all time. Lady Asquith, the Prime Minister's wife, thought that Kitchener 'was a poor general but a wonderful poster'.

Whatever the paper's editorial opinion may have been, its letters page did a good job of encouraging the local chaps to enlist. One letter, published in December 1914 from 'One of the Ettington Lads' was effusive in its praise of life in the army. The food, praised to the hilt, is described in detail: roast meat, salmon, bacon, stews and puddings. Soldiering was, the writer enthused, 'the finest thing I've ever done… and I am having the time of my life'. If the lads back home enlisted they too 'would find it the happiest life going'. Briefly the downside of living under canvas was touched on, but of course that was going to be rectified soon with 'comfortable billets'. For a poorly paid young man, and there were many living in the squalid courts and cramped houses along Great William Street, such letters were persuasive. Many enlisted simply to get fed and clothed.

One month later the *Herald* reported an eventful recruitment day with two companies of the Hampshire Regiment marching round town. A uniformed speaker at the evening meeting demanded: 'is it right that for any man in this audience between the ages of nineteen and thirty-eight to be here and not with them?' pointing to the soldiers present in the room. Then he described the brutality of the Belgium occupation after which he demanded, 'Are you going to do your bit and go with these soldiers... or are you just going to say three cheers?' There was a hint of threat: 'if we find that you will not come with our begging then we shall fetch you... enlist now, and the men in khaki will direct you'. At such meetings the message was reinforced by leaflets stating that 'God's help' would ensure victory, ending with the exhortation: 'enlist now!'

By March 1915, the initial excitement had flagged. The *Herald* announced that not enough young men were stepping forward. The town was visited by Lieutenant Colonel Gretton who was responsible for recruitment for the Southern Command. Both he and the Mayor, Mr Fred Winter, were at a loss as to why men were not enlisting in sufficient numbers. Mr Arthur Lacey, a local business man, thought that visiting villages with a military band would 'enthuse' young farmers. He added that young men needed to know that the government had relaxed the rules regarding teeth. Those refused because of their bad teeth could now reapply.

If the country needed more men, with or without good teeth, Emmeline Pankhurst, the leader of the militant WSPU (see Chapter 20) had an answer. In 1915 she worked closely with Lloyd George, under the Ministry of Munitions, to organise a demonstration of over 30,000 women. They carried banners exclaiming 'Mobilise the brains and energy of women'. But some questioned this idea. The editor of the *Herald* challenged the wisdom of allowing women into 'occupations that hitherto were considered closed to them' and had the foresight to ask: 'what will happen to these women at the end of hostilities' and the prospect 'of a very grave economic problem that will arise' when men return to reclaim their jobs. He was worrying unnecessarily: the employment of women returned to one third of the total working population, exactly the same as before the war.

Sensitivities about women's involvement remained, especially if they were to be close to battle. Dr Elsie Maud Inglis was told by the War Office to 'go home and sit still' when she offered 1,000 trained nurses for the front but she didn't - her offer was accepted by the French government instead. Against similar opposition Miss Margaret Damer Dawson fought to create the Women Police Volunteers. Her women police officers were accepted reluctantly and they had no power of arrest and could only deal with women, children and refugees. But they paved the way for women police officers even though at the time they were seen as working only for the duration of the war .

The Voluntary Aid Detachments

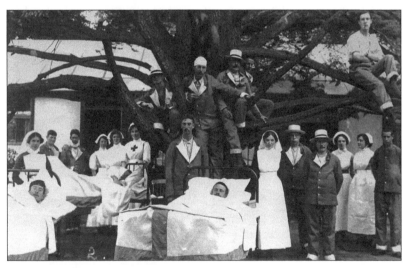

Fig 59. The VAD hospital at Clopton House 1915

Voluntary Aid Detachments (VADs) were first formed in 1909 when the government realised that there might be a shortage of nurses should the country go to war. Initially organised by The British Red

Cross Society it was able to provide 47,000 volunteers by 1914. Their recruitment was initially resented by professional nurses but once the war started, it soon became obvious that there were simply not enough professionals to cope. Temporary Auxiliary Hospitals were set up around the country in large houses and other suitable buildings, staffed by VADs and managed by a matron.

In Stratford, there was one such unit in St Gregory's Road at Whytegates which operated from May 1915 to February 1919. The house was donated to the war effort by the owner and a total of 946 soldiers passed through its doors. A second unit was opened at Clopton House, home of the Hodgson family. There the soldiers were settled in huts when not out in the grounds (Fig 59).

A third hospital was set up in the Town Hall where forty beds were made available under the chandeliers. However, the injured occupants were later transferred to Whytegates where there was a pleasant garden. Soon there were over 3,000 Temporary Auxiliary Hospitals across the country and soldiers were said to prefer them to the more military main hospitals. The group of VADs photographed in 1916

Fig 60. The VAD Nursing staff at Clopton House 1917/18

(Fig 60) at Clopton House with Matron, Miss Ind and Sister, Miss Shand, look both friendly and competent. Trains brought the injured to Stratford. On 22nd February 1918, the *Herald* recorded the arrival of ninety injured soldiers comprising '61 cot patients and 29 sitters'. This sort of exercise had been repeated many, many times throughout the war and speedy transfer, often in private cars, from train to hospital was essential. The injuries and operations undertaken were recorded in the 'Operations Book'.[116] As one might expect, there were amputations of limbs, and toes due to 'trench foot'. But highest on the list were GSWs, standing for general shrapnel wounds and FBs (foreign bodies).

Women's Voluntary Reserves

A different opportunity to volunteer arose in 1914 with The Women's Voluntary Reserves (WVR). The initiative of two militant suffragettes, it aimed at 'freeing more men for the firing line'. The Stratford battalion, formed in 1916, was led by Mrs Eleanor Melville, wife of Canon Melville of Avonbank (Fig 61). Nationally the WVR

Fig 61. Stratford's Women's Voluntary Reserves 1916

attracted an odd mix and at first appeared to be rather elitist. Initially there were tensions as women of the upper classes found themselves alongside politically active women whom they would rather have avoided. The women observed strict military discipline and wore khaki uniform, which was expensive, at £2 a uniform. There was strong objection to the uniform being khaki, since that was the colour associated with military prestige, and that, some felt, belonged exclusively to men.

However the WVR ended up running canteens, transporting the wounded, camp cooking, store-keeping and providing general motoring support. The Stratford group was praised in the *Herald* for all its good work on nearby farms - but it was also, inevitably, criticised for taking jobs from men thus easing them into the war – which was its aim.

Those not fighting felt an urgent need to get active. Such was the enthusiasm that in 1915 the Public Services Committee was formed to record and co-ordinate all the various groups that sprang up. Almost immediately, the Belgium refugee problem presented an opportunity for 'one to do one's bit'. The Belgian Refugee Committee, chaired by Mr Archibald Flower, took responsibility for housing refugees and some of the finest houses threw open their doors. The Flower family set an example when they opened Hill House off the Warwick Road and more accommodation was created at 'Belgian House' on Guild Street and 'Rowley House' in Rowley Crescent. All items loaned, such as curtains, furniture and crockery, were meticulously recorded in small ledgers as were gifts of potatoes, fruit, butter, money and pots of jam.[117] Fund-raising events were frequent and created a hectic social whirl for the middle classes of Stratford. Such was the whirl of activity that on one occasion Mrs Florence Flower, too exhausted by all her committee work to attend a concert, sent a note of apology along with a ten shilling note.

The Stratford War Sewing Fund

Other groups focussed their attention on the troops. In 1914 Queen Mary allowed her name to be used to promote the work of her 'Needlework Guild'. This inspired many middle class women to sew. As early as January 1915 the Stratford War Sewing Fund, organised by Mrs Florence Flower, had sent 1,600 'comforts' to the soldiers. They misguidedly thought their job was over but by September Florence was writing: 'there seems to be every probability of a second winter'. She and her ladies set to work but they needed more materials. They appealed for money to buy wool, and with the £29 7s 0d raised, bought a further 155 pounds of khaki wool from Mr J C Smith in Wood Street. The nature of 'comforts' might have remained a mystery but for a folder kept by Maud Gem, Florence's meticulous secretary. There we learn that 'comforts' included socks, scarves, mittens, night shirts, bed jackets and pyjamas, and that on 10th December 1915, 500 mittens and 500 mufflers were despatched - along with the Director General's Form No. 221. A different 'comfort' were the leather waistcoats made by the Waistcoat Society from donated coats and capes. The almost constant appeals for more donations in the *Herald* speak of the popularity of these items.

The Women's Farm Labour Committee

Whilst many women knitted and sewed, others got dirty. The employment of women in agriculture had fallen drastically because agriculture, along with mining, was viewed as an unsuitable occupation for women. But by 1917 food shortages changed that thinking and the Women's Land Army, funded by the Boards of Agriculture and Fisheries, came into existence with the caveat that it was 'just for the duration'. Stratford had its own land army, monitored by the Women's Farm Labour Committee, The minutes of the meetings record the farmers' opposition. One farmer wanted the women to 'stay for at least five months' and another resented the time spent 'training them up'. Others refused to participate. Despite some opposition many young women went on to earn the colourful Certificate in Farm Work and their work was of great value to the war effort.

The Cultivation of Allotments Committee

That same year, 1917, the Cultivation of Allotments Committee got under way and Miss Hubbard, then running her school in 12 Mayfield Avenue, was a stalwart member. The Cultivation of Allotments Committee set about auditing land suitable for such use. Nationally the whole idea took off and with one-and-a-half million allotments created by the end of the war - the country was said to be suffering from 'allotmentitis'. Miss Hubbard also supported the Herb Growing Association set up in January 1917. This was not as fanciful as its name suggests. The nation was running low on herbal medicines that had previously come from Europe. The Association decided to produce dried camomile, blessed thistle and henbane from a 'drying shed' in Shakespeare Street but the war came to an end before the good work could really begin.

Fig 62. Gladys Wyatt delivering milk 1916

In a less public way, other women were quietly stepping into new work. Gladys Wyatt did the milk round for her father Frank because Edward, the only son, was away at war. The family lived on Masons Lodge Farm (Fig 62).

In 1917, a short while after that photo was taken, the editor of the *Herald*, in a reversal of his earlier opinion, praised the 'plucky ladies' who were doing valuable agricultural work. In particular he mentioned a young woman delivering milk. Women said that they found a sense of freedom in their new jobs. If they were as happy in their work as Gladys seems to have been, it is easy to see why, after the war, they were often reluctant to return to the confines of domestic life. By 1918, there were 113,000 women working on the land, doing jobs previously reserved for their husbands and brothers. Add to this the number of women working in factories (where they could earn up to three times their usual wage in domestic service), that added up to a lot of reluctant women.

War Tribunals

Whilst the women of Stratford were mending, making, planting and generally doing whatever they could, the war continued its relentless slaughter. The initial enthusiasm for the fight diminished and the government was very soon presented with the problem of maintaining a viable army. With the 1915 National Registration Act it sought to discover exactly how many potential recruits were available. Everyone between the ages of fifteen and sixty-five, who was not in the armed forces, had to carry a registration card. This included women, Fig 63.

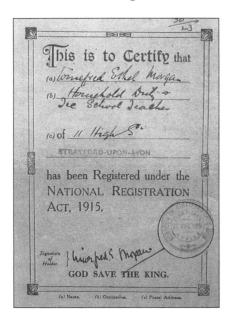

Fig 63. Winifred Morgan's registration card 1915.

The War Office hoped that, by gathering such information, eligible young men would be nudged into volunteering. When that failed, letters were sent to those who had not enlisted suggesting they reconsider in 'the present crisis' as Kitchener 'wants every man he can get'. When that failed, the Military Services Act was passed (January 1916) and from then conscription began and volunteering ceased. Propaganda could only do so much. In January 1916, unmarried men aged between eighteen and forty-one were deemed to have enlisted and it was for them to argue that they should be exempt. To succeed they had to prove that their occupation was of 'national interest' or that they were too infirm. Later, when the number of conscripts was proving insufficient, widowers without children, in that age range, were included. Soon after, married men were also included and the maximum age extended to fifty-one.

In order to manage the conscription process, local war tribunals were set up and hearings for Stratford Borough and the Stratford Rural District were held respectively in the committee room of the Town Hall and the Workhouse board room. Depending on the evidence, the tribunals could grant exemptions ranging from 'temporary', then 'conditional', then 'non-combatant' through to 'absolute', with appeals heard in Warwick.

Stratford Borough hearings had the local brewer Mr Archibald Flower as chairman with Mr Fred Winter, local draper, as his deputy. Assisting them were two councillors Mr Joseph Burke and Mr John Metters. Those sitting in judgement did not find the task pleasant and Mr Charles Couchman, the chairman of the Stratford Rural District Tribunal, said 'it is the most disagreeable job I have ever had to do'. Mr Flower was of the same opinion. At the start there were scathing comments in the local press as to the arbitrary nature of their decisions and public confidence in them was not high.

Early in 1916, Mr Henry Bullard, being a Congregationalist, applied for non-combatant exemption (Chapter 4 described the wrecking of his auction room in 1900). He was eventually court-marshalled and sentenced to imprisonment. Later, in March, Mr William Clark, the manager of Mr Winter's new toy factory won the first of several temporary exemptions. They were gained not so much because the country needed wooden toys but because, of the fifty-three people he was managing, many were Belgian refugees. This argument did not help Miss Marie Corelli, the famous authoress, who was less successful in her attempt to keep Mr Fred Archer, her gardener. She was given a temporary exemption of a month to get her remaining three staff reorganised. Mr Charles Garlick, piano-tuner and music dealer, put up a spirited fight at his appeal, arguing: ' I am practically the only piano tuner in the town and neighbourhood'. This was when his initial absolute exemption on the grounds of ill health had been challenged by the military. He was successful and was not to know that his case would be reviewed again in October 1918. This was when the country was dangerously short of men and his absolute exemption was downgraded to temporary.

Conscription placed immense pressure on small shop keepers so it is not surprising that records reveal many resisting the call to arms. Most stated that the loss of a valued employee (or son) would jeopardise their future. In December 1916, Mr Albert Danks, (*see* Chapter 4 for his stolen duck incident) made the news again with his appeal against the conscription of his eighteen-year-old son, Harold. Danks argued that his fish-hook business could not spare his one remaining son; two others, Arthur and Edgar, were already serving in France and Mesopotamia (now Iraq, and where Edgar was to die a month later). His pleading was less successful this time round and his appeal was dismissed. Mr Henry Bailey, the green grocer on Wood Street, thought he had a good case with his son's 'bad feet and varicose veins' but the tribunal ruled that he was fit enough for 'garrison duty'. It cannot have been easy for Mr Winter to face those he knew well on the bench before him, especially so when he faced Mr Boyden in May 1916. Together, in 1908, they had fought a famous libel case brought by Miss Corelli. Mr Boyden cited his own support for the war effort through his newspaper and requested 'some consideration'. He went on to fight several appeals against his son Rupert's repeated temporary exemptions until the final one, which extended until April 1919, a lucky thing.

In January 1917, when more soldiers were badly needed, married men with families were made eligible for service and Mr George Salmon was brought before Mr Winter. His employer, Mr John Lewis, argued that he needed George to manage his pork-shop and slaughterhouse on Chapel Street. Following lengthy questioning Mr Winter asked if Mr Lewis had thought about employing women to which he replied 'I have one at home I keep pretty well employed'. His case was dismissed. But Mr Lewis continued to appeal and with the help of a solicitor managed to get the last exemption extended to May 1917. Mr Salmon was killed five months later during the 2nd Battle of Passchendaele on 26th October 1917, aged thirty-nine. He left behind his wife Rosa and four children. Conscription was deeply unpopular and divisive. By the end of the war, it accounted for slightly under 35% of the armed forces.

Hoarding, rationing and economy

Meanwhile the food shortage, not helped by the poor harvest of 1916, was causing increased alarm. There was a well-founded fear that essential foods might run out before the autumn harvest. The situation was made worse by hoarding which existed on such a scale that it was difficult for poorer people to obtain a regular supply of basics. To control the situation, hoarding was made illegal under the 1917 Food Hoarding Act and the *Herald* informed its readers that the new Food Control Controller (FCC) in London had the power to search homes. It was under this new legislation that Miss Corelli was brought before the magistrates in January 1918. She had bought far in excess of her permitted allowance of thirty-two pounds of sugar - and it had come from two shops, which was certainly not allowed. She maintained it was to make jam and in fact 470 jars of jam had been produced leaving a mere twenty pounds of sugar in a locked tin in her kitchen. When charged she declared that she was 'a patriot and would never think of hoarding'. The magistrates took thirty minutes to find her guilty and fined her £50 and costs.

Although rationing was seen as the solution by the Government, it was resisted in Stratford and elsewhere. Food tickets were suggested as an alternative. When discussed in the *Herald* the idea went down badly with the paper's readers because they were 'such an un-English system'.[118] Over the weeks so many letters and leaders encouraged economy and thrift that one exasperated reader said he was 'fed up with economy'. In an effort to reduce flour consumption residents were encouraged to collect 'pledge cards' from the Town Hall which, when completed, entitled the resident to wear a purple ribbon showing that they had reduced their bread consumption by one quarter. But by November it was clear that such efforts were not enough. Sir Arthur

Yapp, director of the national campaign for economy, informed the country that the consumption of bread had increased - economy had failed.

When compulsory rationing could be resisted no longer the FCC passed the powers to local authorities to enforce his orders and to do 'as they see fit'. This caused the Mayor, Mr Winter, consternation and he admitted to finding it 'difficult to keep up with the number of orders issued'. However, he was sure that with the help of Superintendent Lee and his police force all was possible - a very misguided notion. The records give a sense of rising panic as the committee reluctantly contemplated the contentious business of prosecuting friends and neighbours. In April 1918, sugar rationing was followed by rationing of meat, butter, cheese and margarine. Superintendent Lee was not as helpful as Mr Winter had anticipated. At an acrimonious meeting of Stratford's FCC, he gave out the opinion that 'Stratford is suffering badly from a lack of moral stamina' and was showing 'moral cowardice'. It all ended with a compromise aimed at smoothing the way for the prosecutions to be conducted by Mr Lunn, owner of 7 Mayfield Avenue. It came as a relief when it all ended in 1919.

The soldiers

All the voluntary activity, for the most part of women, was conducted against a backdrop of waiting, waiting for a letter or a telegram. The letters sent home from soldiers were often constrained in their composition, because letters were censored and because there was an understanding that wives and parents back home needed to be shielded from the reality of war. Mr Eric Winter's letter, sent to his Ma and Pa, is an example. He was stationed in Folkestone and he talked of the weather and of trouble with a set of deserters bound to be sent back to France. He asked, poignantly, if the gramophone was working because he could do with one. It is all couched in light and uncomplaining terms. In 1918, he was thought killed but had been taken prisoner and returned home, thinner but alive.

Mr William Clark's letters, written at the end of the war, demonstrate anxiety about future employment, compounded by frustration at the cumbersome demobilisation process. Mr Clark sent many letters to his former employer, Mr Winter, whose many successful appeals to the war tribunal had delayed his conscription to November 1917. He had been the managing director of Mr Winter's family firm for twelve successful years as well as manager of the more recent toy factory (Fig 2 No. 37). He was keen to get back to work, 'to get out of this lot' and his wife had suffered because she had been obliged to 'take a job'. He requested that Mr Winter completed a 'slip' and stamp it so that he could be released. By 1919 there is a tone of desperation in his letters: it was raining, the men had rioted because the post was erratic and the demob system was unfair and chaotic. Fortunately Mr Winter completed the required 'slip' and Mr Clark returned home and hopefully back to his old job. It would seem that Mr Clark spent almost as much time waiting to be demobbed as he had on active service.

For others there was no home coming, just a small beige envelope containing a telegram. A total of 247 such telegrams arrived in Stratford. Mrs Sarah Wesson (*see* Chapter 12 The Workhouse) lost all three sons Arthur, William and Albert in the space of six months. She received two beige envelopes and her daughter-in-law received the third. Mrs Lucy Sheasby also received two envelopes when she lost Thomas aged twenty and George aged twenty-one. A few years before the war the family of eight were living at 8 Summer Row, a run-down slum by the side of the canal on Great William Street (Fig 2 No. 41) and it is notable that very many young men who lived in that area volunteered at the start of the war. They were members of large families, in low paid jobs and poverty was rife. George, an apprentice builder, volunteered in November 1914 and had fought to win three medals, the Victory, British and Star. When he was killed in late August 1916 Mrs Sheasby received her first beige envelope; the second envelope arrived a year later in September 1917 on the death of Thomas.

The loss of soldiers killed fighting was recognised by the award of inscribed bronze plaques, five inches in diameter. These quickly became known as the 'Death Penny' (Fig 64).

Fig 64. A Death Penny, courtesy P Loe

Mrs Sheasby would have received two if she completed form W.5080. She certainly received one for George, her first born son: his plaque was dredged from the canal in the sixties. This was the busy canal that flowed just a few feet from her back door. She died, aged 80 in 1947. It doesn't take much imagination to think who may have thrown it there.

A local eight-year-old, Florence Robbins, recorded in her diary on the 11th day of the 11th month 1919,

'The anniversary of the Armistice day. The king has asked everybody in our Empire to keep quite still and perfectly silent for 2 minutes at 11 o'clock and think of our glorious dead. Everybody we know was ever so pleased to do so'.

Chapter 23

Legacy

Whilst the Great War continued and Stratford kept busy with its various war efforts, Jane Edwards was living quietly in Leamington Spa. She had taken a while to settle but eventually chose 7 Clarendon Square. This determined woman left Stratford in 1906, probably to escape humiliation after her eldest daughter fell into debt. But having escaped the Stratford gossip, Jane could not escape from the anxiety of war. Like many other grandmothers she would have fretted over her four young grandsons. They had enlisted at the start of the war, and like many other young men, were proud to do so, thinking it would be a short business. She would have waited for news of them but did not live to know their fate. She 'passed gently away' in Clarendon Square aged seventy-five, on the evening of July 18th 1915. Her death certificate, signed by her daughter Ann, gives the cause as *apoplexy* (a stroke) followed by *heart failure*. She was buried in Stratford churchyard beside her husband and young son.

Her former tenants in Russell Court may have read of her death in the Births, Marriages and Deaths column of the *Herald* with mixed emotions. A small entry simply gives her death date, address and that she was the widow of Michael Edwards - no mention of her successful but quite tough life in the intervening thirty-seven years.

The family photograph (Fig 65) was probably taken in the summer of 1915, just before she died. She is sitting to the left with two of her daughters Nellie and Katie (middle standing), her son-in-law (sitting) and four grandchildren Edward, Cecil, Alice and Mary. She wears quite a modern blouse and skirt, but with the hairstyle and neck ribbon of the 1860's, her formative years.

Jane Edwards legacy was twofold. To her daughters, whom she cared for a great deal, she bequeathed sufficient wealth to ensure they could continue to lead comfortable lives (detail in Appendix 4); to the town she bequeathed a quite sizeable number of fine houses, 5

Mayfield Avenue being one of them. She was happy to call them her 'Estate' and she hoped her daughter Ann would extend it. That hope came to nothing just as Mr Keen's hope for his land had been doomed way back in 1790.

Fig 65. Jane Edwards and family c.1914 courtesy John Sirett

But the land that had held Jane's and Mr Keen's interest and ambitions had one last gift - the fascinating 140 years of its history, a history that gives us a unique insight into Stratford. Back in 1775, when, by means of inclosure, Mr Keen consolidated his land holdings, Stratford was a very small, slightly drunken, rather fractious place; today by subtle and gradual steps it has become internationally known and very different and the history of the land shines a light on this process. We watch the land pass from one person to the next and we see the town change before our eyes. From Mr Payton, in his White Lion Inn, who put the town on the cultural map with his 1769 Garrick Jubilee celebrations, to the brave women who fought for women's rights and the men who fought a war.

It is a history as patchy and scrappy as the history of any other small provincial English town. Over the one hundred and forty years covered by this book the residents suffered some oppressively harsh laws and at times political and religious differences led them towards riot. But what is also clear is that when the residents had their consciences pricked they united, as with their well organised petition against slavery, nothing but good resulted. Philanthropy of the best kind provided the poor with free medical attention until the government eventually took over and delivered a more reliable and egalitarian service. For many years fear of the workhouse hung like a cloud over the town and many lived compromised lives in the hidden slums. But with the eventual introduction of council housing schemes the slums were eradicated. The intervention of the state in education pushed forward free non-denominational schools and once the dust had settled all the children in town benefitted. When 'Votes for Women' was a national rallying call, the women of Stratford opened a 'shop' and marched. Today the town has different problems but quite remarkably the *Herald* is still around to report them.

And finally to Shakespeare. Back in 1769 the famous Mr Garrick left Stratford 'in a rage muttering curses against an ignorant townsfolk, the unhelpful Corporation and the dirty insanitary town, never to return again' – after inaugurating the idea of literary celebration.[119] It has to be hoped that today when visitors come for the Shakespeare experience they return home with a more favourable impression and perhaps some of them will glimpse the deeper history of Shakespeare's town that lies beneath.

Appendix 1

The Earps of Mayfield Avenue

In May 1911 when Ann Edwards sold 5 Mayfield Avenue to Mr Charles Earp the house became closely associated with a remarkable family. He had already bought the house next door three years earlier. There he provided a home for his mother and two sisters, who for the first time in many years must have felt a sense of security. Although Charles' visits to Stratford were fleeting his sisters settled and feature in Chapters 10, 12, and 16. They, along with their mother, presented themselves as a genteel trio but their earlier lives touched on less palatable aspects of Victorian life. The family can serve as a lively case-study for Victorian life.

The three Earp siblings grew up in the close-knit community of ribbon and silk weavers living on Galley Common, Stockingford, near Nuneaton. Their father Charles inherited a flourishing family silk-weaving business which over the years gradually specialised in ribbon weaving. He and his wife Anna had their first child, Charles Henry, in 1858 and their daughter, Marie Elizabeth Amy, in 1860. However, a few years later something caused the family to leave their business to live in Mold, Flintshire where in 1866 Gertrude Nora was born. Until this time they were a typical middle-class Victorian family, running a successful business producing a product that every Victorian woman wore in abundance. It was probably around this time that they experienced the death or the alienation of Charles, their father, because he disappeared from their lives. Then they only just avoided the workhouse. Charles junior was sent to live with his grandparents back in Stockingford and on leaving school became briefly involved with ribbon weaving. But Gertrude, Marie and mother Anna disappear from census records. It may be that Anna took her girls back to her former home in Ireland.

The intervening years may well have been tough for Anna but by 1881 she was reunited with her son Charles and they were all living in West Bromwich. Anna had become a 'certificated' school mistress teaching in the school next door and Charles was a builder's clerk. The days of wealth and weaving were well and truly over but at least the family were reunited and housed. Unfortunately this was short lived and the family was split once again, possibly because Charles married and moved away. Later he left the country altogether and from then on the three women were left without his supportive income.

The three women had to look to the future and be self-sufficient if the workhouse was to be avoided again. They moved to Kintbury in Berkshire where Marie became the mistress of a laundry. Laundry work was tough and the trade lacked prestige and certainly would not have been their occupation of choice but managing the laundry also provided them with accommodation. Demand for laundry services rocketed for various reasons in the second half of the nineteenth century and Marie's job was therefore secure, if daunting. Laundresses had a reputation for being, tough and hard drinking and were prone to age prematurely due to the chemicals used in the process and the harshness of the work.

While his sisters were sweltering in the laundry, brother Charles must have found his niche because he became a wealthy man. He and his wife Edith are recorded as sailing many times to New York where he had made his home. In the ship's log he is recorded as being a 'manager' employed by US Steel Products. In 1908 he bought 4 Mayfield Avenue allowing his mother and two sisters to establish themselves as three refined middle-class women living 'off private means' in one of the best parts of town. Their harsh life in the laundry was to become a thing of the past.

Gertrude and Marie flourished and threw themselves into good works. Their earlier life with its hard knocks seems to have given them sympathy for the underdog and they became involved with the town's workhouse library. In 1913 Gertrude is reported in the *Herald*, on an almost weekly basis, thanking individuals for their donations of books - in June 1915 it was for 'illustrated papers and magazines' and a 'parcel of Daily Mail'. Maria is frequently recorded as giving generously to the hospital (the photograph of her in Chapter 18 shows her enjoying a fund-raising event). Gertrude became a Justice of the Peace and may have been present when Alfred Danks was caught with his stolen duck (*see* Chapter 4). She was certainly a JP for many years and in 1937 was holding that position along with the heads of powerful families in Stratford.

All four lived well into old age. Anna, their mother, and Maria both died at home, Anna in 1914 and Maria in 1938. Charles died in New York in 1943, and Gertrude left Mayfield Avenue, following the death of her brother, to die in 'Little House', Wellesbourne in 1951 which at the time may have been a home.

Appendix 2

Later Owners of 5 Mayfield Avenue

Jane Edward's daughter Ann planned 5 Mayfield Avenue at the end of 1903. As we already know she probably ran out of money or steam or both when the terrace of seven houses was reduced to just three. She rented the house to Mr Ernest Young and by 1906 Mr Francis Robinson, a grocer's manager, was resident. In May 1911 she sold the house to Mr Charles Earp for £450. He had already bought the house next door (number 4, known as 'Woodside') for his mother and sisters. He was resident in New York and so rented out the property for nearly nineteen years during which time the house became known as 'Lindridge'.

Over the years, owning a home has become both a sound investment and a mark of success. Gradually, and more particularly from the late 1960's early 1970's onwards, renting has come to be seen as a poor option. It is interesting to look at the changing value of No 5.

- In 1930 Mr Earp sold No 5 to Mr Milward for £650. Mr Milward sold on in January 1931, losing £10 in the process.
- Sisters, Misses Gertrude Nellie and Marjorie Ellen Bailey paid Mr Milward £640. The deeds have many alterations because it seems that their father, Mr Walter Bailey, a furniture dealer, was originally the purchaser. However, the sale went through to the sisters and they (or really their father) let the property to a series of people, mainly Reverends.
- In 1948, Mr A B Muir, a manager at the White Swan Hotel, paid the sisters £3,100 for the house and took out a mortgage of £2,250 with The Tewkesbury and District Permanent Benefit Building Society. His stay was brief, and possibly not a happy event.

- Mr Muir paid off his mortgage in March 1950 when he sold the house to Mr William Frederick Hardy, head waiter at a local hotel. Mr Hardy paid £3,400 but his stay was also brief.

- In October 1951 Mr Hardy sold the house to Mr Kenneth Marcus English for £3,600. Mrs Janet English and daughter Lysbeth English were made 'tenants in common' and all three signed the paperwork. When Lysbeth went to live in Vancouver, power of Attorney documents had already been signed which made the sale a straightforward business.

- In 1959 the Hardys sold the house to Mr Michael Lewis Smith, a company director, at a considerable loss, for £2,975. Mr Smith was able to pay off his mortgage when he sold the house in 1962.

- Mr and Mrs William Green from Lowestoft paid Mr Smith £3,350. They lived in the house for eight years, both dying in 1969. Because widowed Mrs Green died intestate her brother, Mr Arthur Hancock, dealt with the sale.

- Mr Hancock sold to Mr Kenneth Dawes, a toolmaker, in November 1970. Mr Dawes paid £5,000 and lived in the house with his family until November 1979.

- In 1979, Mr Martin and Ms Valerie Horton paid Mr Dawes £30,000 for the house and took out a loan with the Nationwide Building Society. In April 1991, because of a split in the marriage, Ms Horton took out a new loan in order to acquire sole ownership.

- In 1998 Ms Horton married Mr Patrick Loe and the couple became joint owners.

Appendix 3

Mrs Edwards' Will

The Edwardian way of death remained, for the most part, Victorian. Jane left a sizeable personal estate, valued at £6,914 5s 4d, for her daughters Nellie and Ann to manage. Nellie sent a card to her uncle William Edwards the day after Jane died using the customary black-edged card and envelope (Fig 66). She also informed him that he would be visited by a Mr Phillips to sort out 'Birmingham Corporation money which comes to us now'.

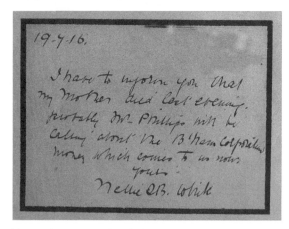

Fig 66. Announcing Jane's death

Jane had drafted her first will in May 1896. She bequeathed all her 'household furniture plate linen china glass books prints pictures jewellery wearing apparel and all other domestic articles and effects in and about my dwelling house' to her daughter Ann, and she appointed two executors to deal with her real estate: Nellie, her daughter, and George Sydney Martin. They were to 'sell call in or otherwise convert into money, my said real estate and residuary personal estate and stand possessed of the monies arising there from'. Surprisingly the proceeds were to be divided equally between Nellie and Ann 'for their use and benefit absolutely'. Her other two daughters, Jane and Katie, were excluded. Jane was trying to protect Ann and Nellie, whom she regarded as vulnerable, Ann because she was unmarried and Nellie because she was twenty-nine and had a three-year-old child whilst married to a husband aged sixty-three - the odds were that Nellie would be left a widow. Meanwhile, daughters Jane and Katie were married and secure, or so it appeared at the time.

The lives of Jane's daughters changed over the years which prompted her to rewrite her will. The new will, written in 1914, was fair and straightforward. As before she left all her 'furniture and domestic effects' along with her 'wearing apparel and personal ornaments' to Ann, her one unmarried daughter. The properties listed were all acquired by Jane once widowed:

- To Jane she left her freehold properties, 1 and 1a Mulberry St, 26 Great William St. and 26 Bridge St, on condition that she 'pays £5 to Ann and pays a quarter share of any debts that I may leave, a quarter of my funeral costs and a quarter of any outstanding mortgages on my properties'.
- To Katie she left two freehold properties in Maidenhead Rd: 'Eastcote' (no. 32) and 'Fairview' (no. 36) and 'Orchards' (no. 11) in Mayfield Ave. This was as long as 'she pays £13 to Ann' and a quarter share of debts as above.
- To Nellie she left Hillcote (no. 42) Maidenhead Road, 'Maryvale' (no. 9) Mayfield Ave and the house adjoining 'Maryvale' (no.10) subject to her paying £6 to Ann a quarter share as above.
- To Ann she left 'Inchcliffe' (no. 40) Maidenhead Road, 'Shirley' (no. 8) Mayfield Ave. and the four cottages to the rear of 'Shirley' subject to her paying a quarter share of any debts, as above.

Two other properties had been sold earlier. They were two Maidenhead Road properties, 'Hillside' (no. 38), sold to her daughter Ann in 1910 and 'Broadview' (no. 34), sold to Mr Hinton in 1904.

In addition to inheriting Jane's properties, her daughters had benefitted, over the years, from property previously owned by their father but managed jointly by Thomas Durant and Jane as trustee. Later in 1892 when he renounced his interest Jane's three sons-in-law took on the duty and the properties were distributed. They were:

- The Mason's Arms and two houses in College Ln, sold in 1892 by the new trustees.
- Numbers 41 and 42 Henley St. given to daughters Jane and Katie in 1896. A later arrangement had Jane owning both.
- Wellington Terrace on Birmingham Rd given to Ann and Nellie.
- 'Elm Cottage' on Maidenhead Rd and all the surrounding land given to Ann in 1911.
- Ely St property and Russell Court given Katie in 1912.

The cottages in Gaydon and the four houses on the Birmingham Road built by her father and where she had spent her childhood, were sold at some point by the trustees. It can be seen that over the years Jane had control or ownership over a remarkable amount of 'real estate' in Stratford.

Appendix 4

Mrs Edwards' Daughters

The Edwards girls' lives were long, with very many years lived as widows in much the same way as their mother. Following her death they were well provided for. However during their early lives they showed a remarkable ability to survive, with varying degrees of success. It should be noted that success more than often involved shops.

Jane Olney

Jane, the eldest daughter, fell into debt and was probably the cause of her mother leaving town. She had at first been the daughter who appeared to be the most successful. In 1882, she married Mr Thomas James Olney, a 'master tailor', and the couple began their married life rather well at 26 Bridge Street, the building that had been her mother's successful drapery (Fig 67).

Fig 67. Widow Olney's shop on Bridge Street 1899, first awning, right side

To enable this to happen Jane had moved, with her three other daughters, into 'Elm Cottage' on Maidenhead Road. Soon Thomas was also calling himself a 'hatter'. Unfortunately he died on the 24th December 1898, leaving his thirty-nine-year-old wife with heavily mortgaged property and no source of income. From then on it all went very wrong. With the help of her solicitor Jane promptly called in all outstanding accounts, threatening court action for non-compliance. Compelled to leave the shop she moved into Elm cottage, her mother's property (who moved out and up the road) and started her own career running a boarding-house, eventually owning her own premises. But whilst doing this she hugely overspent and by 1906 her outstanding accounts were out of control. Trust in her willingness to pay up evaporated and in the same year she was publicly exposed at two meetings of her creditors in the Red Horse Hotel on Bridge Street (Fig 68 now Marks and Spencers). There they subjected her to questioning, so convinced were they that having had a wealthy father and husband she was surely in possession of inherited money.

Fig 68. The Red Horse Hotel c.1890

It should be remembered that debt was something extremely shameful. The thirty-four creditors agreed to send their final bills. A sample:

- To Mr Frank Organ, furnishing, £44 17s 5p.
- To Mr Joseph Mitchell, baker, £13 9s 1d.
- To Mr George Edmonds, butcher, £2 8s 0d.
- To Mr H Cresswell, fishmonger, £5 18s 0d,
- To Mr James Henson, another butcher, £20 4s 0d.

- To Mr George Boyden, newspaper proprietor, £4 16s 6d.
- To Mr Fred Winter, haberdashery, £5 18s 3d.
- To Mr Henry Bailey, fruit and game, 14s 3d.
- To Mr Arthur Lacey, hardware, 5s 9d.

Jane's public exposure prompted her mother to move, and not just further up the road but to 57 The Parade, Leamington Spa. Her daughter understood that the move was to be for about a year but Jane senior never returned.

After her ordeal by debt, daughter Jane continued to earn a living in Stratford with her boarding-houses, firstly in Guild Street and later in John Street (Fig 2 Nos. 24 and 26). In 1914/15 she retired and moved to 17 Old Town and in 1923 she settled in her Henley Street shops, (Fig 69 central property), opposite Shakespeare's Birthplace (Fig 2 No. 29). There she traded, along with her son, or leased the properties which mutated over the years from a café into a sweet shop, an antique shop and the 'Shakespeare Gift Shop'. The tourists had arrived and Jane was in the centre of things. She died in 1951 aged ninety-two.

Fig 69. Jane Olney's Henley Street shops c.1910

Nellie White

Nellie was born on the 10th March 1867. In the family photograph (Fig 65) she is standing second from the left. Of all four girls, Nellie's life was the quietest. She married Stephen White in Bristol on the 21st July 1890. He was a retired Inland Revenue officer and was aged fifty-seven, a lot older than twenty-three-year-old Nellie. He is seated next to Jane in the photo. They lived in Sheep Street, Shipston-on-Stour and in 1893 had their only child, Norman. He enlisted in 1914 and went immediately to serve as a marksman in Lucknow, India, where he spent the entire war. By 1911 Nellie and Stephen had moved to Leamington Spa, possibly to be closer to Jane, who was perhaps in failing health. Later they retired to Herne Bay where in 1924 Nellie was widowed. In 1926 she sold Hillcote and her Mayfield properties and, later, Wellington Terrace and eventually returned to the Midlands. She settled at 45 Lordswood Road, Birmingham to be with her widowed sister Ann. Nellie died in 1959, aged ninety-two, having spent thirty-five years as a widow

Katie Dorothy (Baughan/Sirett)

Katie was born in 1870. In the photograph (Fig 65) she is standing, second on the right. She met her first husband when he was boarding in her mother's house. Mr Alfred Henry Baughan, from Stow-on-the-Wold, is variously recorded as a farmer or a solicitor. He and Katie married in 1891 at the Baptist Chapel in Stratford when he was twenty-eight and she twenty. They settled in Sheep Street, Charlbury, near Chipping Norton, where Alfred gave up both farming and the law to become a draper. In 1893 they had their only child, Cecil Henry (standing to the right in Fig 65). Alfred died in 1902 and two years later Katie remarried to thrice-widowed Mr Caleb Sirett, thirteen years her senior. Caleb moved into Katie's home, bringing with him three children - Alice, Mary and Edward - and an eventful past. The son of a poor agricultural labourer he began his working life, aged nine, as a plough boy and over the years had been a tea dealer, a grocer and a Baptist Minister. On marriage he gave up on the ministry and became a draper/dealer.

When war was declared Cecil, Katie's son by her first husband, enlisted with the Royal Warwickshire regiment but he was discharged three years later, in June 1917, as sick, having been seriously injured. Caleb's son Edward also enlisted in 1914, illegally because he was just fifteen. He served for the whole of the war and was killed in action on the 4th November 1918 just one week before the end of the bloodshed. He is standing in uniform at the back of the family photograph (Fig 65) with his two sisters seated at the front. Caleb died in 1925, aged seventy-three, leaving just £122 14s 2d.

Katie meanwhile held onto her inherited wealth, as the law then allowed. Widowed for a second time, she eventually moved to Birmingham where she lived with her son Cecil. She died in August 1962, at 45 Lordswood Road, aged ninety-two having moved along the road to be with her sister. Her estate stood at £9,428 6s 0d. It must therefore be assumed that, like her mother, she had already passed on property to her only son Cecil. He died just four months after his mother leaving a sizeable estate of £23,429. 4s. 10p to his widow. Lois Baughan was Jane Edwards' grand-daughter-in-law and she chose to leave Birmingham to live out her last days in 11 Mayfield Avenue. This was the house that Jane had planned back in 1905 and is situated opposite number 5, the inspiration for this book. She died there in 2000 at the age of ninety-seven.

Ann Jubb

Ann, the baby of the family, was the daughter everyone expected to stay unmarried and stay at home but she surprised them all, initially by not staying at home and then by marrying Mr Joseph W Jubb in 1921. He was a sixty-year-old retired certificated teacher and she, by then, was forty-eight.

Ann was of an independent mind and by the time she was eighteen she had taken herself off to live with her married sister, Nellie, in Shipston-on-Stour. There she earned her living as a photographic re-toucher, which was quite a new occupation. She was artistic and decided to take her profession more seriously when she returned to Stratford to live with her mother; she studied at the Birmingham School of Art and, as reported in the *Herald*, won most of the honours on offer there. She went on to become a teacher at Shipston-on-Stour School of Art and remained there for some years. She became a well-known local artist and in 1902 exhibited three paintings in London at the *'Art and Industrial Exhibition'*. She then settled in Bristol where she advertised her private lessons and became a portrait artist.

At one point, Anne owned thirteen properties and a considerable swath of prime development land off Maidenhead Road. This was the property her mother had given her in the misguided hope that she would continue to develop the 'Estate', but gradually she sold off her inheritance. When widowed in 1947 Ann went to live in Birmingham to be reunited with her sister Nellie. She died in Birmingham in 1967 aged ninety-four, the last surviving daughter.

Bibliography

Most of the information contained in this book has been obtained from original documents found in the archives of the Shakespeare Birthplace Trust. Additional biographical detail has been obtained from Ancestry and the International Genealogical Index. The following were also information sources.

Acton Dr Lesley, (2015) *Growing Space: A History of the Allotment Movement,* Five Leaves

Anderson Michael, (1971) *Family Structure in 19th Century Lancashire*, Cambridge University Press

Auchterlonie Mitzi, (2007) *Conservative Suffragists. The Women's Vote and the Tory Party,* Taurus Academic Studies

Bayne Powell Rosamond, (1951) *Travellers in 18th England,* J. Murray

Bearman Robert, (2007) *Stratford upon Avon: A History of Its Streets and Build*ings, Stratford on Avon Society.

Bearman Robert, (1974) *Stratford-Upon-Avon Social life and Customs. Education in the 19th. Century pamphlet,* Stratford Birthplace Trust

Bearman Robert, editor (1997) *The History of an English Borough,* Sutton Publishing

Boughton John, (2018) *Municipal Dreams, The Rise and Fall of Council Housing,* Verso

Burchardt Jeremy, (2002) *The Allotment Movement in England 1793-1873,* Boydell & Brewer

Caldwell Michael J, (2000) *For King and Country, The Fallen of Stratfor*d, self- published

Crawford Elizabeth, (2006) *The Women's Suffrage Movement,* Routledge Group.

Deelman Christian, (1964) *The* Great *Shakespeare Jubilee,* Michael Joseph Ltd

Fletcher Ronald, (1978) *The Biography of a Victorian Village,* Batsford

Glazier Mary, (1996) *Essay on Common Lodging Houses in Chester 1841-1871*, self-published

Guy Winter's family collection

Head Peter, (1961) *Putting out in the Leicester Hosiery Industry*, University of Leicestershire Archaeological and History Society

Higgs Edward & Wilkinson Amanda, (2016) *Women's Occupation and work in the Victorian census, Revisited, History Workshop Journal*, Liverpool University Press

Holloway Gerry, (2005) *Women and Work Since 1840*, Routledge

Jones Mark, (1998) *The Mobilisation of Public Opinion against the Slave Trade and Slavery 1787-1838*, University of York Department of History

Kelly's Directory

Kohler Carl, (1983) *History of Costume*, Dover Publications

McFarland Patricia, (1995) *Six Town Clerks of Stratford on Avon 1762-1894*, University of Warwick Dissertation

Noakes Lucy, (2005) *Women's Military Services in the First World War*, Routledge

Olusoga David, (2016) *Black and British, A Forgotten History*, Macmillan

Page William, (1908) *The Victoria History of the County of Warwickshire*, Constable

Parson and Bradshaw Directory

Pigot's Directory of Warwickshire

PO Directory

Ragland Johnny, (2004) *The Hidden Room*, Kingston University

Rosen Andrew, (2012) *Rise up Women*, Routledge

Saunders Janet, (1988) *The Anatomy of Madness*, Routledge

Slatter's Directory

Spennell's Directory

Spinks Philip and Julie, (2017) *First World War Services Tribunals, Warwick District Appeal Tribunals 1916-1918,* Dugdale Society Vol. 50

Spinks Philip, (2014) *First World War Military Service Tribunals 1916-1918,* Ruskin College

Spinks Philip, (2015) *Warwickshire History Vol 3,* Warwickshire Local History Society

Stanley and Bolton Almanak

Styles Philip, (1945) *A History of Stratford upon Avon,* Victoria County History

Swanwick Helena Maria, (1935) *I Have been Young,* V Gollancz

Turner, Dr David, (2011) *Slavery and the Financing of Britain's Early Railway System: A consideration,* History Lab

Walvin James, (1999) *The Slave Trade,* Sutton Pocket Histories

Walvin James, (2007) *A Short History of Slavery,* Penguin Books

Webster's Dictionary, New Edition 1862

White's Directory

Willis, Dr Sam, (2016) *British Highwaymen,* BBC production

Wilson A N, (2002) *The Victorians,* Hutchinson

www.britishnewspaperarchive.co.uk

www. recordoffice@warwickshire.gov.uk

www.ucl.ac.uk/lbs Legacies of British Slavery Ownership

roadstomodernity.com Company of Merchants Trading in Africa,

postalmuseum.org

https://hammond-turner.com Hammond & Turner Button People,

www.thisismoney.co.uk/historic-inflation-calculator

www.open.ac.uk/Arts/history-from-police,

https://digital.library.lse.ac.uk/collections/thewomenslibrary

www.victorianweb.org/authors/corelli/kuehn5.htmlfet.uwe.ac.uk

https://fet.uwe.ac.uk/conweb/house_ages/council_housing/print.htm

www.nationalarchives.gov.uk

www.forces-war-records.co.uk

www.qaranc.co.uk History of British Army Nurses,

www.bfi.org.uk The British Film Institute archives,

https://www.telegraph.co.uk/.../Women-voted-75-years-before-
they-were-legally-allowed...

Endnotes

All references are to the BPT Archives unless stated otherwise.

1   BR15/18/107
2   BR15/18/107
3   BRU15/18/109
4   ER2/534(vii)
5   DR444/6/4/3
6   ER17/15/1
7   ER2/534(ii)
8   ER1/139
9   ER1/139
10 SBT Databases
11 The Great Shakespeare Jubilee by Christian Deelman p.260
12 BRU2/7 Book G
13 ER25/3/16/1
14 ER10/2/31
15 ER10/2/34
16 BRT/4/4/2
17 ER10/2/118
18 *Herald*, 11th-25th May 1877
19 *Herald*, 10th-31st March 1877
20 BRR11/7/14
21 DR18/17/37/12
22 ER5/488
23 BRU15/17/88
24 BRU2/7
25 ER10/3/157
26 UCL Database
27 DR198/7
28 DR745/12
29 SAVP12/4/1
30 ER10/2/232

31 *Herald*, 6th February 1872
32 *Herald*, 13th July 1888
33 *Herald*, 30th November 1888
34 *Herald*, 22nd April 1892
35 *Herald*, 16th January 1891
36 DR 149/154/167
37 DR1073/1/1/11
38 DR1073/1/1/1
39 BRU15/17/239-292
40 ER13//3/1
41 DR165/1254/10
42 ER10/3/99 and 100
43 BRR8/1/4
44 BRR2/1/1
45 QS24/J/617 Warwick Records Office
46 BRR8/1/5
47 *Herald*, 16th-2nd September October 1864
48 BRR13/1/9
49 ER11/10/26
50 BRR37/6/71
51 BRR67/3
52 *Herald*, 19th-12th February March 1886
53 BRR67/13
54 Poll Register 1820, page 13
55 ER10/2/54
56 ER/11/14/18
57 ER11/13/30
58 DR1073/1/1/14
59 BRT8/198
60 BRT8/238
61 ER11/6/12
62 ER11/6/11
63 ER10/5/239
64 ER/11/20/15

65 Census 1911
66 CR1664/298 and 618 Warwick Records Office
67 DR324/3/2
68 ER10/3/119
69 DR165/414
70 DR165/427
71 DR165/415
72 DR243/53
73 DR165/418
74 DR27/130
75 ER25/3/1/1
76 DR243/55/1 and DR243/55/3
77 BRR2/5/1 and 2
78 *Herald,* 3rd March 1881
79 DR1073/1/1/17
80 DR574/728
81 DR253 & DR324/1/1
82 DR907
83 DR317/74
84 DR253/2
85 DR253/1
86 DR325/2270
87 DR27/511
88 DR325/2232
89 DR324/2/17
90 DR324/2/22
91 CR1664/30 Warwick Records Office
92 CR1664/30 Warwick Records Office
93 CR1664/623 Warwick Records office
94 CR1664/667 Warwick Records office
95 ER1/2/88
96 ER11/32/79
97 ER3/2488 and ER3/2487
98 DR27/127

99 DR395/52

100 *Herald*, 2nd Aug 1861

101 DR27/508

102 DR165/597 1869-1900

103 *Herald*, 16th October 1908

104 *Herald*, 10th February 1911

105 *Herald*, 17th-March 10th February 1911

106 *Herald*,, 3rd March 1911

107 DR730/36

108 *Herald*, 24th February 1911

109 DR730/29

110 BRR2/18/1

111 *Herald*, 9th December 1870

112 *Herald*, 23rd April 1908

113 *Herald*, 23rd April 1909

114 *Herald*, 5th April 1912

115 DR650/44 and DR650/76

116 DR1216/3

117 BRR71/26/1/4

118 *Herald*, 16th March 1917

119 The Great Shakespeare Jubilee by Christian Deelman p.263

Index

BV - #0006 - 221119 - C0 - 229/152/14 - PB - 9781912419760